HOW TO READ THE HOLY FATHERS

A Guide for Orthodox Christians

FR. JOSEPH LUCAS

ANCIENT FAITH PUBLISHING
CHESTERTON, INDIANA

Published by:
Ancient Faith Publishing
A Division of Ancient Faith Ministries
1050 Broadway, Suite 6
Chesterton, IN 46304

Unless otherwise noted, Scripture quotations are taken from the New King James Version, © 1979, 1980, 1982 by Thomas Nelson, Inc. Used by permission.

The Sayings of the Desert Fathers: The Apophthegmata Patrum: The Alphabetic Collection, trans. Benedicta Ward. Copyright 1975 by Cistercian Publications, Inc. © 2008 by Order of Saint Benedict, Collegeville, Minnesota. Used with permission.

Cover design by Amber Schley Iragui. Cover image (evangelist): bpk Bildagentur / Bayerische Staatsbibliothek / Art Resource, NY. St John the Evangelist, Gospel of Lorsch, Heidelberg, 11th century. Cover image (hand of God): Heather MacKean, inspired by 12th century Hand of God from Sant Climent de Taüll.

ISBN: 978-1-955890-76-2

Library of Congress Control Number: 2024949350

In this book, Fr. Joseph Lucas gives us a balanced approach to seeing the Church Fathers through an array of personalities, styles, and historical contexts, which nonetheless comprise the one single choir of Holy Tradition. He presents an ideal to aim for in approaching these holy figures, an ideal most of us often fall short of. The framework presented therefore traces a clear and reasonable path to follow as we progress toward Christ in the footsteps of these holy examples.

—JONATHAN PAGEAU, host of *The Symbolic World*

Father Joseph Lucas's engaging treatment of what our Orthodox Fathers valued reads not as a distant and removed tome for scholars but rather as a primer for those seeking to understand the foundations of our Orthodox Faith. Yet this is no trite read, but one built on the breadth of the Fathers' own vision, one that asks its lectors to move beyond a mere "Sunday School" level knowledge of the Faith and to the depths and riches that await the serious student. Giving first a necessary introduction on who the Fathers are (not just ecumenical teachers), when they lived (not just in the distant past), how they should be used (not for quote mining), and what one must endure to grasp them (no cursory or breezy reading of the internet), Fr. Lucas's wonderful text takes its readers through the genres of writing and the categories of study that the Fathers themselves devoted their lives to, and thus opens the gate to a world that a lifetime cannot exhaust, and one ever-new, no matter how ancient. Organized around the matters of chief importance to the Fathers—subservience to Scripture and the Rule of Faith, the life of prayer, the defense and teaching of the Faith, the devotion to the Liturgy—the text pulls one in from its very first pages. This text gives to those involved in catechesis (whether receiving or teaching) an excellent tool as an introduction to our Faith.

—DR. CYRIL GARY JENKINS, Director, St. Basil Center for Orthodox Thought and Culture, Eastern University

In this accessible volume, Fr. Joseph Lucas has done a great service for the Holy Orthodox Church. The contemporary reappropriation of the patristic corpus, even at our parish level, is marked by great zeal. All too often, unfortunately, this has been a zeal not according to knowledge. In *How to Read the Holy Fathers*, Fr. Joseph outlines an approach to reading and applying the writings of the Fathers that will help the reader avoid the all-too-common pitfalls and fallacies that distort, rather than elucidate, the light of patristic wisdom—an approach that can allow this light to shine more brilliantly in the lives of today's Christians.

—V. Rev. Dr. Stephen De Young, author of *The Religion of the Apostles*

If you are just beginning to read the Fathers, this is the book for you. It offers a road map to the rich variety of authors, genres, and historical periods within patristic literature. It also provides a concise introduction to the theological and philosophical background, as well as practical advice for how to read the Fathers in an Orthodox spirit. If you want to learn to drink from the deep well of patristic wisdom, this is an excellent place to start.

—Dr. David Bradshaw, Professor of Philosophy, University of Kentucky, and author of *Aristotle East and West*

Orthodox Christianity intimately knows that God was, is, and forever shall remain "the God of our Fathers." Father Joseph Lucas introduces the Orthodox reader to the beauty and significance of this fact with care and lucidity. Moreover, he goes a step further and acquaints us with the Fathers themselves, and encourages us both to read their works and, more importantly, to imitate their lives. As you read this book, may you be inspired to exclaim, again and again, and with an ever-greater depth of understanding, the petition that closes every Orthodox service: "Through the prayers of our Holy Fathers, Lord Jesus Christ our God have mercy upon us, and save us. Amen!"

—V. Rev. Dr. Alexis Torrance, Archbishop Demetrios Associate Professor of Byzantine Theology at Notre Dame University

I would like to express my sincere gratitude to all those who have fostered my love and understanding of the Church Fathers over the years (in order of when we first met): Fr. Patrick (Carpenter), Fr. John Maxwell, Dr. Christopher Veniamin, Dr. Harry Boosalis, Fr. Andrew Louth, Fr. John Behr, Fr. Matthew Baker (of blessed memory), Fr. George Dragas, and Fr. Bogdan Bucur. Their encouragement and guidance inspired me to dedicate my life to the study of these luminaries, an endeavor that has enriched my spiritual life in so many ways. I would also like to thank those patristic scholars whom I never had the pleasure of meeting but whose writings have influenced me greatly: Fr. Georges Florovsky, St. Dumitru Stăniloae, and Fr. Georgios Mantzaridis. I also thank my parishioners and students whose many questions have helped me to frame patristic theology in ways comprehensible to the laity. Last but certainly not least, I thank my wife, Preoteasa Irina, for supporting my writing efforts.

"Do not remove the ancient landmark
Which your fathers have set."
Proverbs 22:28

Contents

Part 2: Application

Introduction

I WAS TWENTY-FIVE WHEN I first encountered the Church Fathers in earnest. As I began to read their writings, I was instantly drawn into a world that was ancient but surprisingly new. It was an experience like the one a woman described upon first discovering patristic thought through the writings of Fr. Seraphim Rose, saying it was "like drinking pure water after wading in muck."[1] I have since spent more than half my life studying their thought—for both personal edification and academic purposes—and have struggled to follow their shining example (however imperfectly). The one thing I have come to understand is that Orthodox Christianity cannot exist without the witness and solicitude of its saints.

The Orthodox Church is deeply rooted in tradition. Her doctrines, practices, and texts have been handed down, generation to generation, for two millennia. These traditions are not simply a fixed set of customs but a living inheritance embodied by the faithful in each particular time and place. What connects an Orthodox Christian today to those who lived in the past is a shared worldview that encompasses everything we say and do: our theological tenets, our asceticism and spiritual practices, our participation in communal worship and the Sacraments, and our practice of God's commandments. When we

---

1   Seraphim Rose, *Orthodoxy and the Religion of the Future*, 4th ed. (St. Herman of Alaska Brotherhood, 1999), xv.

1

follow this way of life, we are guided by the clergy—our bishops and presbyters—who received their authority through another sort of handing down, a succession of ordination we can trace back to the apostles themselves. But the clergy are not alone in this task; the entire Church is entrusted with the preservation and dissemination of the Orthodox Christian Faith.

The movement of Tradition through time may be an organic, historical process, but it is not blind: It is always guided by the Holy Spirit. Thus we may refer to our patrimony as Holy Tradition because it is not merely the fabrication of humans. And the same Spirit that preserves and enlivens Holy Tradition also raises up certain individuals from within the Church to be its expositors and defenders, a specific class of those called to be saints (from the Latin *sancti,* or "holy ones"). God imparts wisdom to them because they love and serve Him with all their heart, all their soul, all their mind, and all their strength (Mark 12:30). We refer to these men collectively as the Holy Fathers (or Church Fathers) because, like parents overseeing a household, they act as wise caretakers of the Faith. Their lives, and the works they have left us, are a testimony to that authentic Christian religion established by Jesus through His apostles. Simply put, if we want to engage and embody Holy Tradition, we must necessarily encounter the Fathers.

In recent decades, reference to the Fathers has become commonplace in Orthodox parishes, due in large part to the academic study of these luminaries, known as patristics, that rose to prominence in the twentieth century (from the Latin word *patres,* for "fathers"). Scholars like Fr. Georges Florovsky invited us to "return to the Fathers" in a way that seeks to apply their wisdom to the concerns of our own age.[2] Orthodox seminaries began to offer specialized courses in reading

---

2   See his "Patristics and Modern Theology," reprinted in *Diakonia* 4, no. 3 (1969): 227–32.

and interpreting the Fathers, immersing future priests in the treasures of the patristic library. And now quotations from the Fathers
appear everywhere—in sermons, on the internet, and in almost
every published book about Orthodoxy. But while the field of patristics (sometimes called "patrology") has been essential to the revival
of the Fathers in our time, we must be careful to distinguish it from
the theological and devotional use of their texts.

A faithful study of the Fathers will necessarily diverge from the
academic approach, not that one is always opposed to the other but
they have different aims. Scholars seek to understand the historical
development of ideas. In order to fulfill this task, they must complete the important and difficult work of producing reliable texts and
translations from the best manuscripts available (more on this later).
Although we benefit from their endeavors, our goal as disciples of
Christ is to acquire the mind of the Fathers, not view them from without as objective or "scientific" observers. Hence, as we come across
academic opinions, we should be wary of theories that would couch
the Fathers within a framework of doctrinal evolution or would
impose modern psychological, sociological, or political interpretations on them. Only a careful and well-informed reader can separate
the wheat from the chaff.

The recent emphasis on the Fathers in Orthodox theology has
also resulted in a backlash from some scholars who envision a post-
patristic age. Whatever they mean by this is often unclear, and fortu-
nately such views remain outliers in the Orthodox world. In response,
we must assert that any version of the Faith that rejects or dimin-
ishes the importance of the Church Fathers severs the golden chain
of Holy Tradition that continues into the present, and thereby dis-
torts the timeless truths of Christianity. We cannot bypass or move
beyond the Fathers. If we are to make sense of them, and of our Faith,
we must take them seriously. It is necessary to read their writings
with the same care we read the Holy Scriptures, always being careful

not to twist their words to our own purposes. When we read them correctly, their writings open up to us another world in which biblical passages, liturgical hymns, doctrinal treatises, and ascetical practices come together as a cohesive whole. We begin to see through their eyes and are able to move past the dichotomies we cling to with our modern (or postmodern) minds, delving more deeply into Orthodox Christianity and discovering greater meaning for our lives. Without the Holy Fathers, we swim in a shallow pond; but with them, we dive into the depths of the sea.

The idea for this book emerged from my work in sharing this patrimony with my parishioners and college students. In fact, this book is not intended for an academic setting; instead, it presents the Fathers to the average Orthodox Christian reader with the hope that all will be able to taste of this great bounty. In part 1, I offer guidance in choosing which books to read, unpacking the texts, and avoiding pitfalls that lead to false interpretations or application. Then, in part 2, we examine the various patristic literary genres together and look closely at examples of each from specific saints. Throughout our expedition I encourage you to enter into a relationship with the Fathers through prayer and imitation of their lives. As we unlock this vault of spiritual riches, may the saints' fervent intercessions guide us.

PART 1

Methodology

CHAPTER 1

Meet the Fathers

Who Are the Fathers?

WHEN WE REFER TO THE inheritance of the Holy Fathers, we generally mean the collections of writings certain saints have left to the Church that, over time, have been endued with authority within the community of the faithful. This includes homilies, letters, treatises, hymns, poetry, biographies, biblical commentaries, ascetical guides, liturgical manuals, historical accounts, lists of canons, and more. These texts were frequently quoted by later writers and often compiled into collections called *florilegia* (anthologies containing excerpts of earlier works). Already by the time of St. Athanasius the Great (†373), theologians were citing the authority of their forebears when they explained or defended orthodoxy. In his *First Letter to Serapion*, St. Athanasius writes, "Let us look at the very tradition, teaching, and faith of the catholic Church from the beginning which the Lord delivered, the Apostles preached, and the Fathers preserved; upon which the Church is founded."[1] The convocations of the great ecumenical councils affirmed the witness of the past by

---

1   St. Athanasius, "Ad Serapion," in *The Letters of Saint Athanasius Concerning the Holy Spirit*, trans. C. R. B. Shapland (Epworth Press, 1951), 133–34.

reference to "the holy and approved Fathers." And by the eighth century, St. John Damascene (†749) took for granted the absolute necessity of deferring to his predecessors, commenting, "We do not change the everlasting boundaries which our Fathers have set, but we keep the tradition just as we received it."[2]

Perhaps the earliest mention of the Fathers as a reference point comes from Titus Flavius Clemens (Clement of Alexandria, †215), traditionally believed to be the founder of the famed Catechetical School of Alexandria. He states, "We call 'fathers' those who have taught us."[3] The Fathers were, first and foremost, teachers of the Holy Tradition that they themselves received. They were responsible for embodying the "good deposit" (2 Tim. 1:14 [translation mine]) entrusted to them, and then for delivering it to others. But we should not see this process as something like passing a baton, the transfer of something static and dead. St. Irenaeus of Lyon (†202) correctly referred to the Church's patrimony as a "living deposit."[4] We may envisage it as something akin to bread-baking. When an apprentice at an artisanal bakery is ready to venture out and start their own business, their master may gift them their first active colony of yeast. They are then responsible for nurturing it—keeping it alive and healthy that it may thrive. If they do this properly, it will become the source of leaven for every beautiful loaf they produce. And someday, perhaps many years later, they will gift a portion of this yeast to their own apprentice—and the cycle continues.

In the same way, the Fathers nurtured the apostolic deposit they inherited through their asceticism and pursuit of virtue, passing on to

---

2   St. John Damascene, "Apologia of Saint John Damascene Against Those Who Would Decry the Holy Images," in *Three Treatises on the Divine Images*, trans. Andrew Louth (SVS Press, 2003), 69.

3   Clement of Alexandria, "Stromateis," in *Ante-Nicene Fathers*, trans. A. Cleveland Cox, vol. 2, *ANF* 2/5:299.

4   St. Irenaeus of Lyon, "Against Heresies," in *Ante-Nicene Fathers*, trans. W. H. Rambaut, vol. 1, *ANF* 1/81:458.

the next generation live embers rather than cold ashes. They became wise teachers because they were humble students first. They not only received the Faith through an intellectual transmission but were transformed by it, such that whatever they offered to others was real and not abstract. They were not merely philosophers who examined ideas about God through rational analysis. As St. Gregory Palamas (†1359) pointed out, "It is said that 'every argument has a counter-argument,' but who can argue with life?"[5] Having been immersed in the Truth and changed by the power of God, the Fathers could properly convey this reality to others. At times they descended to the level of their students in order to explain the Faith, often finding new ways to present old teachings. At other times they soared above into the lofty contemplation of divine mysteries, offering others a glimpse into heaven through beautiful prose (which explains why so many excerpts from their writings were later taken up and incorporated into the Church's hymnody). Yet in everything they did they remained true to "the faith which was once for all delivered to the saints" (Jude 1:3).

Through the writings of the Fathers, we benefit from the sagacity they gained through personal experience. Summarizing this understanding, Metropolitan Hierotheos of Nafpaktos writes:

> In the Church, as St. Gregory Palamas says, there are "those initiated by experience" and those who follow and revere these tested ones. Thus if we do not have our own experience on these matters, we must nevertheless follow the teaching of those who see God, the deified and experienced saints. It is only in this way that we have the mind of the Church and the consciousness of the Church. Otherwise we open the path to self-destruction in various ways. We must constantly

---

5   St. Gregory Palamas, *The Triads: In Defense of Those Who Practice Quietude*, trans. Peter A. Chamberas (Newfound Publishing, 2021), 93.

believe and confess "in accordance with the divinely inspired theologies of the saints and the devout mind of the Church."[6]

The Holy Fathers are those who fall within the first category: those who have stood before God. As for us, we begin in a third category—those who neither know God directly, nor experience Him vicariously through the saints. But we may slowly be initiated into the second group by studying patristic works and applying their wisdom to our own lives. Even if we never behold the glory of God during our lifetime, we can glimpse it through the eyes of the Fathers.

The Fathers were also shepherds tasked with protecting the flock on behalf of the chief shepherd, Jesus Christ. Unlike many modern theologians who work within the constraints of the academy and see their research as a contribution to the ever-expanding domain of human knowledge, the Holy Fathers envisaged their vocation as selfless service to Christ and love for their fellow humans. The basis of their teaching and preaching was always a fervent desire to assist the faithful in their journey toward salvation. They avoided provocation and dangerous theological speculation because they feared harming those entrusted to their care. Their defense of the Faith did not originate from a fear of conceptual diversity but from a duty to guard vulnerable souls from the spiritual adversary who "walks about like a roaring lion, seeking whom he may devour" (1 Pet. 5:8). In addition, they were not cloistered off somewhere in an ivory tower, and they did not stand aloof from the people; rather, they walked side by side with them as both spiritual guides and fellow pilgrims.

Most often, the Fathers were shepherds in the specific sense: ordained clergy appointed to guide the Church in an official capacity. For this reason, we rarely speak of Church Mothers. Of course, we

---

6   Metropolitan Hierotheos of Nafpaktos, *The Mind of the Orthodox Church*, trans. Esther Williams (Birth of the Theotokos Monastery, 1998), 238–39.

do not ignore the plethora of female saints in the Orthodox calendar, nor their works (indeed, they have left us a handful of writings).[7] Even so, we give preeminence to those pastors accountable to their flock because of their ecclesial position. Their vocation, confirmed by the laying-on of hands, shaped their thoughts and deeds as they labored to bring the people of God together in oneness of mind. To accomplish this, they had to become "an example to the believers in word, in conduct, in love, in spirit, in faith, in purity" (1 Tim. 4:12). Like the father of a large family, they exercised their spiritual leadership over the "household of God" (Eph. 2:19), representing Christ in the midst of the faithful.

Historians will often lump individuals into the category of patristic who would not be considered such by the standards of the Orthodox Church. They will include writers who did not align with Orthodox doctrine, or who veered into heresy later in life. While there may be useful information in such figures that helps to contextualize the Fathers, we cannot take these texts as authoritative. For example, Tertullian—perhaps the first Christian to write exclusively in Latin, beginning in the late second century—started out his career as a devout member of the Church in Carthage. Some of his early writings encapsulate well the doctrine and practices of Christian life there. In fact, a famous saying is derived from his *Apologeticum*: "The blood of the martyrs is the seed of the Church." But around the year 207 he converted to the Phrygian heresy, led by a self-proclaimed prophet named Montanus. This calls into question the utility of Tertullian's works, even those documents he wrote prior to his apostasy. The same can be said of Origen, whose theology was posthumously condemned

---

7   For example, we have a few aphorisms from Amma Syncletica, Amma Sarah, and Amma Theodora in the *Sayings of the Desert Fathers*; the travelogue of the nun Egeria; the teachings of St. Macrina as recorded by her brother St. Gregory of Nyssa; the letters of St. Olympia to St. John Chrysostom; and the surviving hymns of St. Kassiani.

for problematic philosophical ideas, and the historian Eusebius of Caesarea, who later aligned himself with the heresy of Arianism.[8]

Orthodox readers today may not benefit from imbibing the works of such men, especially if they lack a skilled guide to point out what is spiritually dangerous. How will they be able to notice subtle distinctions in the text? How will they recognize that Origen used a faulty definition of the word "age" (in Greek, *aiōnos*) that affected his view of the final judgment? Or that Diodore of Tarsus subtly divided Jesus Christ into "two Sons," thus laying the groundwork for the Nestorian heresy? Unless you are pursuing graduate studies in history or theology, where knowledge of the entire historical milieu is necessary, there is little utility in poring over authors who diverged from Holy Tradition unless they are already digested by trustworthy authors and purged of heretical ideas.

When we speak of "Holy Fathers," we assert that their lives were a reflection of God's holiness, not merely that their writings were theologically sound and traditionally oriented. The Church has always understood that "You will know them by their fruits" (Matt. 7:16), and with the addition of Acts to the New Testament canon, the Church established a direct correlation between the way a person lives (their actions) and the things they produce (their writings). The biographies (or in Latin, *vitae*) of the Fathers reflect their devotion to God, and such works also become a source of inspiration and teaching. They serve as evidence as to why we venerate a particular Father. In addition, a saint's inclusion in the liturgical calendar of the Church, confirmed by the process of canonization, serves as an official imprimatur of his or her holiness.

More importantly, we must not see the Fathers as separate from the whole of Holy Tradition, especially the Scriptures. Although

---

8   His early work *The History of the Church* is perhaps the only text read widely in Orthodox circles.

the Bible certainly represents the core and foundation of Orthodox doctrine and practice, the same Spirit that spoke by the prophets and indwelt the apostles also illumined the saints in every era of the Church. Perhaps the only difference between the Scriptures and the many volumes of patristics texts is that the latter have never been edited into one seamless unit. To be sure, authoritative collections have been published—such as *The Philokalia* and *Evergetinos*—but these remain the exception, not the rule. By and large, the body of patristic literature remains unedited and unvarnished. And yet within we encounter the same prophetic and apostolic ethos as their antecedents. The Holy Fathers are the bridge between the ancient biblical authors and we modern Christians.

Historical Periods of the Fathers

ONE COMMON MISCONCEPTION WE MUST be aware of is the view that the Church Fathers comprise only those Christian writers who lived in antiquity. Operating on this premise, scholars divide the Fathers into linguistic camps and designate set periods of flourishing. For example, they refer to the Greek Fathers, ending in the eighth century; the Latin Fathers, ending sometime prior to the Great Schism in the eleventh century; and the Syriac Fathers, consisting of a handful of writers including St. Ephrem the Syrian (†373) and St. Isaac of Nineveh (†700). According to this construct, antiquity represents a golden age of patristic activity, later succeeded by either scholasticism in the West, or a period of unoriginal repetition in the East. However, there are problems with such facile classifications.

First, as already mentioned, the Orthodox Church does not purport every Christian writer from antiquity to be a Father. A slew of texts survive that, while not necessarily heretical, lack any real authority within the Church because they do not reflect divine inspiration. Whether we refer to the *Divine Institutes* by Lactantius, the

Commentary on Thirteen Pauline Letters by Ambrosiaster, or the *Commentary on the Apostles' Creed* by Rufinus, such texts are not included among the authoritative writings of the Holy Fathers, even though they are old (and perhaps helpful in filling out our historical impression of early Christianity). Antiquity alone is not enough. Later theologians rarely if ever referenced some authors because they fell short of the mark. Failing to embody the breadth and depth of Holy Tradition, they were often preserved primarily for historical purposes.

Second, if we truly believe that the Holy Spirit does not abandon the Church, we must assert that the age of the Holy Fathers cannot end until the "glorious appearing of our great God and Savior Jesus Christ" (Titus 2:13). The same Spirit who granted wisdom to St. John Chrysostom (†407) in Antioch and Constantinople also spoke to St. Sophrony of Essex (†1993) in modern Great Britain. What is remarkable about the Fathers is the consistency of their profession of faith over so many centuries, even if they expressed it in different tongues and with terms appropriate to the time period they lived in. While we may lend greater authority to earlier writers due to their proximity to the apostolic age or because they lived during the period of the great ecumenical councils, it would be incorrect to set their works in opposition to more contemporary theologians such as St. Nikolai of Žiča (†1956) or St. Paisios the Athonite (†1994). If we speak of the Fathers in the past tense, it is because their authority is only confirmed after their repose (in the same way we glorify them as saints). This process of wide-scale recognition is itself a movement of the Holy Spirit within the Church.

Without denying the continuity of the Fathers into our own time, we can still outline a historical scheme based on the context in which each generation flourished. We can also trace a development of terminology and the pronouncement of official dogmas over time, which is always cumulative (the more recent never replacing or contradicting what is older). This is not to contravene the biblical assertion that the fullness of divine revelation was disclosed to the apostles and handed over to the early Church. As Christ promised, the Spirit would lead His disciples into "all truth" on Pentecost (John 16:13). Yet it was necessary that the Fathers continually unpack the implications of the apostolic deposit in each era; to clarify and crystallize the language used in theology; and to defend the Faith when those who misunderstood the paradox of God's interaction with humanity challenged it. When theological issues faced them, the Fathers strained to find just the right words with which to frame the Faith. Once the Church writ large affirmed these expositions, they entered into the lexicon of Orthodoxy.

The earliest patristic texts are compiled under the heading "Apostolic Fathers." Some of the works included in this category are those of St. Clement of Rome (+99), St. Polycarp of Smyrna (+155), and the anonymous Shepherd of Hermas. These Apostolic Fathers provide us a link between the New Testament documents and the Church of the early second century. Perhaps the most important set of texts within this collection is the seven letters of St. Ignatius of Antioch (+107), written shortly before his martyrdom, which influenced all successive generations of Christians. The holy hierarch presents a liturgical vision of Christianity—inspired by his teacher St. John the Apostle and Evangelist —with his vivid descriptions of the liturgical life that existed in each local Christian community. He is the earliest writer to define the Church as "catholic," following the Aristotelian definition of "wholeness." What makes the Church in Antioch, or in Smyrna, or in Ephesus whole is that a local bishop presides over the eucharistic worship, surrounded by his presbyters, deacons, and all the faithful, and that the consecrated bread and wine, having become the Body and Blood of Christ, is "the medicine of immortality."[9]

---

9 St. Ignatius of Antioch, "Epistle to the Ephesians," in *The Apostolic Fathers*, ed. and rev. Michael W. Holmes (Baker, 2002), 151.

From the middle of the second century through the beginning of the fourth century was a patristic period often referred to as that of the ante-Nicene Fathers (which means, "before the Council of Nicaea"). These saints lived through a tumultuous time marked by regular cycles of local and state-instituted persecutions such as those imperially decreed by Decius (249–251), Valerian (257–260), and Diocletian (303–313). In spite of the constant threat of arrest and execution, writers such as St. Justin the Philosopher (†165), St. Irenaeus of Lyon, and St. Theophilus of Antioch (†183) penned brilliant treatises. Their defense of Christian doctrine prompted them to adopt new terminology and provide vivid descriptions of the Faith that would later become standard. For example, St. Theophilus gives us the first recorded use of the word "Trinity" (in Greek, *triados*) to describe the three divine Persons.[10] And St. Irenaeus presents us with the earliest account of how apostolic succession works, including the first explanation as to why the Church reads only from the four Gospel books de rigueur. Others, like St. Cyprian of Carthage (†258) and St. Methodius of Olympus (†311) faced heresies and schisms within the Church: the former wrangling with the Novationists and the latter correcting the ideas of Origen. Before the Edict of Milan established a policy of toleration toward Christians in the Roman Empire in 313, the ante-Nicene Fathers were true heroes of the Faith who exemplified the self-sacrificial life of Christ through their deeds. They paved the way for a renaissance of patristic flourishing.

The era that begins with the Council of Nicaea in 325 may be described in one of two ways: either as one long epoch that comes to an end with the fall of Constantinople in 1453; or as two periods, the first half being the conciliar age—that of the great ecumenical councils—coming to a close with the restoration of icons in 843,

---

10 Theophilus of Antioch, "Apologia ad Autolycum," trans. Marcus Dods, *ANF* 2/3:101.

and the second half being the post-conciliar age. Either description is apt, because on the one hand there is an incredible consistency in theological expression throughout the entire epoch; but on the other hand, the challenges after the great councils differed vastly from those of earlier centuries. When we refer to this period in toto, we will use the term "Byzantine Fathers" to describe these luminaries, as the majority of them were Greek-speaking clergy and theologians living in the eastern half of the Roman Empire (which scholars refer to today as the Byzantine Empire). Over the course of a millennium, the Byzantine Fathers distilled and crystallized Orthodox Christianity such that our religion cannot be understood apart from them.

In the conciliar period, there are a host of noteworthy saints whose works have survived. The aforementioned St. Athanasius looms large as a major influence upon the First Ecumenical Council, which affirmed the divine equality of the Father and Son. The preaching, writing, and tireless pastoral work of the three Cappadocian saints—St. Basil the Great (†379), St. Gregory the Theologian (†390), and St. Gregory of Nyssa (†395)—were pivotal in shoring up the Faith in the period before and after the Second Ecumenical Council when the divinity of the Holy Spirit had been called into question. The luminance of St. Cyril of Alexandria (†444) shines upon the Third, Fourth, and Fifth Ecumenical Councils, which all dealt with the proper interpretation of the Incarnation of Christ. The transcendent teaching of St. Maximus the Confessor (†662) was exonerated at the Sixth Ecumenical Council, where the bishops agreed that Jesus' human will is distinct from His divine will yet acting in perfect harmony with it. And the Seventh Ecumenical Council took up St. John Damascene's powerful defense of iconography as a traditional proof of the Incarnation. Over the course of four centuries, the Church withstood numerous heresies because of these and many other Holy Fathers.

In the post-conciliar period of the Byzantine Empire, there were four preeminent Fathers who set the tone for their successors. The first of these is St. Photius the Great (†891). Perhaps his greatest achievement was to expose a new heresy that had emerged in the West: the *filioque* (a Latin phrase meaning "and the Son"). By unilaterally inserting these words into the Nicene Creed, Latin theologians had disrupted the doctrine of the Trinity. A century later, St. Symeon the New Theologian (†1022) flourished. His emphasis on a believer's direct, personal experience of God, and the necessity of ascetical and mystical contemplation by even the laity, challenged the laxity and complacency that had become commonplace at that time. In the fourteenth century, St. Gregory Palamas built on this approach, defending the ancient practice of stillness and prayer known as hesychasm (which he in turn connected to the way God operates within creation). And just before the fall of Constantinople to the Ottoman Turks, St. Mark of Ephesus (†1444) stood up to Roman Catholic attempts to subjugate the Orthodox Church to the Pope of Rome, hence providing an early critique of late medieval Western theology and innovations such as purgatory and papal supremacy.

There were also a handful of important Latin Fathers who flourished during the conciliar period, such as St. Ambrose of Milan (†397), St. Augustine of Hippo (†430), and St. Gregory the Dialogist (†604). In an Orthodox reading of these saints, we must take caution not to set them in opposition to the Byzantine Fathers; yet the reader should be alert to differences in terminology and theological expression. Since the vast majority of Church Fathers wrote in Greek, and because the creeds, councils, and major doctrinal disputes were elaborated in Greek, the massive body of Greek patristic texts holds preeminence. In a sense, we read the Latin Fathers through the lens of the Byzantine Fathers. In due time, political realities led to a gradual estrangement of the Roman Church from the Orthodox Church. This was a slow process, marked by tragic events such as the Great

Schism of 1054 and the sack of Constantinople by Western Crusaders in 1204. As this process unfolded, Western European theologians would transition away from a common patristic discourse, and the theology of the Latin Fathers gave way to the philosophical art called scholasticism.

A brief word should also be said about the Syriac Fathers. Although they were few in number, the impact of their work is enormous. Their tongue was a dialect of Western Aramaic, similar to the language spoken in first century Palestine by Christ and His apostles. And the version of the Bible they used was called the Peshitta, a translation into Syriac from Hebrew and Greek manuscripts that began in the second century and was completed by the fifth century. Because of the Syriac Fathers' unique linguistic and geographic milieu, their writings reflect a more Semitic vision of Christianity, overflowing with poetic and biblical imagery. With the eventual translation of their writings into Greek (and Slavonic) beginning in the fourth century, they would broadly influence the later biblical exegesis and hymnographical tradition of the rest of Orthodoxy.

After the capture of Constantinople by the Ottoman Turks, many modern commentators assert that the Orthodox Church entered into a dark age. Islamic hegemony certainly did stifle Christian education and religious expression in the Mediterranean basin. But schools to the north of the Balkans—in what is today Romania, Ukraine, and Russia—became the new centers of theological thought. However, the prosperity of Western Europe also became a lure for many Orthodox students. They traveled to Italy, Germany, and France to study at Roman Catholic universities. And after Martin Luther sparked the Protestant Reformation in AD 1517, yet another theological approach was introduced to Eastern Christians sojourning in the West. Such interactions often adversely affected the theologians of that time. They began to define Orthodox dogmas using terminology and symbolism borrowed from other traditions, and at times even adopted

Roman Catholic or Protestant ideas cut from whole cloth. For example, St. Nicodemus the Athonite (†1809) purchased an indulgence (called a certificate of absolution) from an Orthodox bishop, mimicking a Roman Catholic practice only officially employed by the Church of Constantinople after 1727.[11] Some Orthodox scholars in the twentieth century would look back on this period as the Western Captivity.

This "pseudomorphosis" of Orthodoxy (as it has been dubbed) would not prevail.[12] The ethos of authentic patristic thought was always hidden just beneath the surface. Although St. Nicodemus was indeed a man of his time, and would often read Latin texts for inspiration, he also began compiling the most important Byzantine spiritual texts into an anthology called *The Philokalia* ("Love of the Beautiful"). His contemporary to the north, St. Paisy Velichkovsky (†1794), then translated these texts into Russian and disseminated them throughout the Slavic lands. The work of these two men inaugurated a revival of Orthodox patristic theology in the eighteenth and nineteenth centuries, a movement which continues unabated to the present day.

During the past two centuries, modern Fathers, coming from diverse cultural and linguistic backgrounds, have joined the ranks of their predecessors. In the Russian Empire prior to the Bolshevik Revolution (which included what is now Ukraine, Belarus, and Latvia), luminaries such as St. Seraphim of Sarov (†1833), St. Philaret of Moscow (†1867), St. Theophan the Recluse (†1894), St. Ignaty Brianchaninov (†1867), and St. John of Kronstadt (†1909) captured the imagination of the people. In Romania, there was St. Calinic of

---

11 Christos Yannaras, *Orthodoxy and the West*, trans. Peter Chamberas and Norman Russell (Holy Cross Orthodox Press, 2006), 95–97.

12 "Pseudomorphosis" is the term Fr. Georges Florovsky employed to describe the influence of Western religion on the Orthodox Church beginning in the fifteenth century. See his *Ways of Russian Theology* (Nordland, 1979), 33–37.

Cernica (†1868), St. Cleopa of Sihăstria (†1998), and St. Dumitru Stăniloae (†1993); in Greece, St. Kosmas the Aitolian (†1779), St. Nektarios of Aegina (†1920), and St. Joseph the Hesychast (†1959); in Serbia, St. Nikolai of Žiča and his disciple St. Justin Popović (†1979); in the Church of Antioch, St. Joseph Damascene (†1860); and in Georgia, St. Gabriel the Fool for Christ (†1995). There are also a few American saints who have left us various patristic texts, including St. Innocent, Enlightener of Alaska (†1879), and St. John Maximovitch (†1966).

As the Church lumbers forward through the centuries, new theologians and spiritual guides continue to be revealed. Modern elders such as Fr. Philotheos Zervakos (†1980) and Fr. Seraphim Rose (†1982) may soon join the ranks of the saints. And brilliant minds such as Fr. Georges Florovsky (†1979) and Elder Aimilianos of Simonopetra (†2019) may one day be held up as universal teachers of Orthodox Christianity. As their writings are gradually encountered and evaluated, the Spirit will determine to what extent they shall take root in the garden of the Church. Only time will tell if their contributions will be ranked among those of the Holy Fathers.

The Works of the Fathers

In order to better understand the writings of the Holy Fathers, it is helpful to classify their works according to certain genres. Although such arrangements may be arbitrary at times— recognizing that some works might overlap multiple categories—the majority of patristic texts indeed may be grouped in such a manner. The largest category of texts is biblical exegesis, which consists of orally delivered homilies or written commentaries that examine the Holy Scriptures and unpack their meaning. The largest collections of exegesis belong to St. John Chrysostom, St. Cyril of Alexandria, and St. Augustine of Hippo. Other categories of patristic literature include doctrinal treatises, apologetics (defenses of the Faith), ascetical literature, correspondence, and biographies. All of these are sources of instruction, whether for theological purposes or to enable the faithful to live a pious life. The authors of manuals that emphasize spiritual or ascetical guidance are often called the Neptic Fathers (from *nēpsis* in Greek, meaning "watchful"). The various collections of *apophthegmata* or aphorisms of the Desert Fathers are included in this category. Although originally written for monastics, such texts are a fountain of inspiration for all Christians.

Another category of patristic writings are those texts used for devotional purposes when the Church gathers to worship, including hymns, liturgical texts, and hagiography. Hymnography includes the various texts sung or chanted during the services. Liturgical texts include all of the service books used by the clergy, readers, and singers during a service. In many cases, the authors of hymnographical and liturgical texts are unknown to us; we may only possess the finished products collected into books such as the *Hieratikon*, the *Horologion*, the *Menaia*, and the *Octoechos*. A few notable exceptions include the Akathist of St. Romanus the Melodist (sixth century), the Paschal Canon of St. John Damascene, and the Holy Wednesday hymn of the nun St. Kassiani (†865). Hagiography is sometimes considered a broad category, encompassing every type of biographical source. However, specific collections of these texts, such as the synaxaria, are read aloud during liturgical services and therefore possess greater authority. The use of all such devotional texts is governed by various typika, or manuals, that explain how to assemble and coordinate worship services throughout the year. These books are also the product of the Fathers, known and unknown, and thus reflect the doctrine and praxis of the Church.

In addition to texts used *in* worship, the Fathers also produced commentaries *about* worship. A tradition of exploring the symbolic meaning of the Church's services began with the *Corpus*

Areopagiticum of St. Dionysius the Areopagite and the subsequent *Mystagogia* of St. Maximus the Confessor. Often, these works provide an elaborate allegorical explanation of the various prayers and physical movements of the clergy. In addition to providing the reader with spiritual edification, such texts are also important for scholars as they piece together the patterns and rubrics of early Christian liturgical worship.

The final category of patristic works consists of various lists of canons. In antiquity, a *kanon* referred to a cane or rod used for measuring, and eventually it took on the meaning of a guideline, rule, or standard. For example, the official list of books included in the Bible came to be called a canon. Lists of canons are collections of guidelines that originate from either a single author or by agreement of bishops at a council. The *Canons of St. Basil the Great* are an example of the former, while the decrees of the ecumenical councils are an example of the latter. Canons may include official dogmatic statements by which all believers are bound, pastoral canons the clergy use to guide their flocks, or administrative canons hierarchs use in their governance of a diocese. As a rule, canons are not like civil laws. Their application is limited to those in communion with the Church; they are never repealed (though a later canon may supersede an earlier one); and they are always intended for good and unto the ultimate salvation of the faithful, not for punishment. Because canons are not intended for general audiences, we will not examine this literary genre in depth.

Not every category of patristic texts is suitable for the average reader to explore, or at least not without a guide. The biblical commentaries of St. Cyril of Alexandria can easily overwhelm the modern exegete with rich allegories that challenge modern ideas about interpretation. The doctrinal treatises of St. Maximus the Confessor will likely confuse someone unfamiliar with standard Greek philosophical terms. And the rigorous ascetical instructions contained in the *Ladder of Divine Ascent* by St. John Climacus (†649) might even drive a spiritual neophyte to despair. When approaching the writings of the Holy Fathers, it is often best to start small and work our way up to more complicated texts over time. A suggested reading list is included in Appendix D of this book, categorized from beginner to advanced based on complexity. When in doubt, seek out help from those more adept at reading the Fathers, including publications by Orthodox scholars and guidance from your local parish priest.

The Harmony of the Fathers

MODERN READERS WHO FIRST APPROACH the Holy Fathers often unintentionally paint them with a broad brush. They assume the Fathers to be monolithic, a singular group of inspired writers who thought and expressed themselves in identical ways. Other readers err to the opposite extreme, believing the Fathers to be absolutely unique individuals who each represent a very different mindset and motivation. The via media between these two poles is to envision the Fathers as something like a choir. Although each saint was exposed to different educational and historical influences, had a unique personality, and possessed his own palette of various innate and spiritual gifts, all were inspired by the same God. The gift of the Holy Spirit does not override the formation and talents of an individual but rather purifies and sanctifies that general human nature which subsists as the unique person we later recognize as a saint. Conformity to the image of Jesus Christ (see Rom. 8:29) entails transformation of the heart, not a banal or superficial imitation.

The distinctive voice of a Church Father is heard when we interact with a specific text he wrote. Through close and careful reading, we come to appreciate the author's writing style, including diction and syntax. We may glean some of his influences, including other writers he favorably quotes or those he opposes. Gradually, we enter into the thought-world of the saint, seeing (in some small part) the majesty of divinity and the purpose of human existence through his hallowed imagination. Yet it is only after we apply this same approach to numerous other Fathers—from different historical and cultural milieus—that we begin to understand how each of these saints refracts the light of Christ in his own way. Although diverse, their voices blend together in perfect harmony.

A story from *The Sayings of the Desert Fathers* illustrates this reality:

It was told of a brother who came to see Abba Arsenius at Scetis that, when he came to the chapel, he asked the clergy if he could visit Abba Arsenius. They said to him, "Brother, have a little refreshment and then go and see him." So, because Arsenius' cell was far away, they sent a brother with him. Having knocked on the door, they entered, greeted the old man and sat down without saying anything. Then the brother from the chapel said, "I will leave you. Pray for me." Now the visiting brother, not feeling at ease with the old man, said, "I will come with you," and they went away together. Then the visitor asked, "Take me to Abba Moses, who used to be a robber." When they arrived, the Abba welcomed them joyfully and then took leave of them with delight. The brother who had brought the other one said to his companion, "See, I have taken you to the foreigner and the Egyptian; which of the two do you prefer?" "As for me," he replied, "I prefer the Egyptian." Now a father who overheard this prayed to God saying, "Lord, explain this matter to me: for your name's sake the one flees from men, and the other, for your name's sake, receives them with open arms." Then two large boats were revealed to him on the river, and he saw Abba Arsenius and the Spirit of God sailing in the one, in perfect peace; and in the other was Abba Moses with the angels of God, and they were all eating honey cakes.[13]

---

13   *The Sayings of the Desert Fathers: The Alphabetical Collection,* trans. Benedicta Ward (Cistercian, 1975), 17–18.

When we read the aphorisms of either St. Arsenius or St. Moses, we simultaneously experience both convergence and dissimilarity. On the one hand, it is obvious they serve the same Lord, are members of the same Church, and seek the same ultimate goal: salvation. But on the other hand, their personalities shine through the text, reflecting two different methods of achieving the same end. Together they reveal a greater expanse of the Kingdom of heaven.

As you read the works of the Fathers, take your time and enjoy the message embedded in each text. Listen carefully to what the author conveys to you, to your mind and heart. Do not rush through, as though you are searching for sources to finish a term paper due by week's end. And as you transition to another text, or another author, remain open to differences in expression in order to appreciate the text in its own right, and not simply for how it supports what you have previously read. In time, the consonance and congruity of the Holy Fathers will come into focus, and the patristic chorus will become a sweet serenade to your soul.

CHAPTER 2

*How **Not** to Read the Fathers*

B EFORE WE CAN BEGIN TO delve more deeply into a proper
reading method, it is best to draw attention to things we should
avoid. The goal of the reader should be to draw meaning out of a
patristic text. When done properly, this is called "exegesis," which
refers to both the process of interpretation and the content of the
interpretation itself. However, many well-meaning readers walk away
from a text either thoroughly confused or holding false conceptions
about its meaning simply because they began with false assumptions.
In order to avoid this dilemma, they need a reliable tool kit, filled
with techniques and resources that assist them in discovering meaning. This tool kit is called a "hermeneutic." Simply put, a solid hermeneutic generally equals good exegesis. Without hermeneutics we are
left to decipher the text on our own, which often leads us to impose
our biases upon the Church Fathers. In this chapter we will approach
the problem from the other end by looking at what happens when we
read a text blindly, thereby demonstrating the importance of establishing a proper hermeneutic.

The Problem of Eisegesis

COMPETENT SCHOLARS AND PEOPLE WHO work in an academic setting readily acknowledge that it is impossible for anyone to put aside every bias and become absolutely objective and neutral while conducting research. Whether we are devising a science experiment, analyzing the data of a sociological study, or reading a historical text, we automatically interpret information through the lens of our training, experiences, and personal ideology. This is especially acute for an Orthodox Christian who approaches a patristic text because the Holy Fathers loom large as sources of our religious doctrine and practices. But while we may never attain absolute objectivity, we can begin by recognizing the biases we possess and then accounting for them. In addition, we can make sure our presuppositions are shaped by reliable information and tempered by an objective and agreed-upon method in order to reduce undue influence on our interpretation.

Whenever we impose our biases upon a text it is called "eisegesis." For example, a hot topic today is the debate between those who espouse the theory of evolution and those who adopt young-earth creationism (as first formulated by American evangelicals). Many Orthodox Christians have entangled themselves in this debate, taking one side or the other and thus forming an a priori opinion. With this presupposition in mind, they may begin to comb through patristic texts looking for evidence to support their views. However, this does damage to the original intent of the texts. Whichever side of the debate the reader falls on, both assume certain modern, materialist, scientific concepts that they are imposing upon the original authors. Not only is this approach highly anachronistic, it also prevents the reader from entering into the mind of the Holy Fathers and seeing the world through their eyes.

Even with the best attempts to remain neutral, ideology will affect our interpretation, and we cannot counter our personal biases unless we first examine what they are. This requires a bit of brutal honesty. For example, perhaps you are a convert to Orthodox Christianity from another religious confession. If so, it is highly likely you will subconsciously carry baggage from that other tradition that will influence your reading. Or perhaps you subscribe to certain political or philosophical ideas that inform your worldview. And beyond these specific biases, we all are adversely influenced by the age we live in. As modern readers we will naturally impose contemporary concepts upon these ancient texts. The way we perceive the world is completely affected by the scientific materialism that saturates our culture. Rather than seeing the world symbolically and theologically as the Fathers did, we look for facts and data and mechanisms. As a wise man once told me, we moderns bow down to the explanation.

When we search out and acknowledge our biases, we are able to approach the text with a more open mind, ready to receive what God desires to communicate to us through his saints. It is good to second-guess ourselves and to assume we might be getting it wrong. A strong dose of intellectual humility goes a long way in this regard because it prevents us from misreading.

However, eisegesis can occur even when we approach the Holy Fathers with the best of intentions. One way to help us read with less bias is to keep in mind the common saying that says, any text without a context becomes a pretext. In other words, we are not ready to read a patristic text until we understand something about the author and his milieu. We can remedy this by studying the historical period he lived in and by understanding the major events that occurred at that time. We should also read a biography of the saint and try to understand the place and culture he occupied. And once we have a sense of who the author is, we should then research the text itself: What sort of work is it? Who was it written for or to? What was the author's purpose in writing? If we do not yet know the answers to these questions, we are not yet prepared to tackle the text.

Just as important as how we read a text is how we use it. We must be careful not to abuse the patristic inheritance by co-opting it for our own purposes (such as winning an argument or engaging in unnecessary polemics with others). One of the best ways to avoid this problem is to eschew proof-texting. At a very basic level, this practice entails quickly perusing a text to extract short passages which prove our point. In such instances the original context is completely ignored or misunderstood because the reader has failed to take ample time to see the whole picture. Many Orthodox Christians decry evangelicals for doing this with the Bible yet do the exact same thing with the Church Fathers.

Even so, not all proof-texting is this facile: Indeed, some readers take additional care to understand something about the context before they extract a quote. But even then there remains the problem of removing an idea from the patristic corpus as a whole to make it stand alone. For this reason we must adhere to the rule known as *consensum patrum*, the "consensus of the Fathers." As St. Vincent of Lerin (+445) explained:

> Moreover, in the catholic Church itself, all possible care must be taken that we hold that faith which has been believed everywhere, always, by all. For that is truly and in the strictest sense "catholic" which, as the name itself and the reason of the thing declare, comprehends all universally. This rule we shall observe if we follow universality, antiquity, and consent. We shall follow universality if we confess that one faith to be true, which the whole Church throughout the world confesses; antiquity, if we in no wise depart from those interpretations which it is manifest were notoriously held by our holy ancestors and fathers; consent, in like manner, if in antiquity itself we adhere to the consentient definitions and determinations of all, or at the least of almost all priests and doctors.[1]

---

1   Vincent of Lerin, "Comminatory," in *NPNF* 11:132.

This unanimity of voice is what distinguishes Holy Tradition from a private opinion (in Greek, *theologoumenon*). An individual saint may, from time to time, express ideas or hypotheses based on their personal experiences, learning, or influences that do not reflect official ecclesial doctrine or practice. Sometimes a certain imprecision in their writing is due simply to the fact that certain dogmas had not yet been clarified by the Church. For example, we cannot accuse the ante-Nicene Fathers of faulty Trinitarian theology because they do not use the terms "Person" (*hypostasis*) and "essence" (*ousia*) as the ecumenical councils later defined. In addition, we must remember that no one is born a saint: He or she undergoes the same lifelong process of sanctification that all Orthodox Christians are called to. This means that texts written in their youth may not reflect the wisdom and clarity of old age.

All of this is to say that, before we quote the Holy Fathers, we should have a firm grasp on where the text falls within the entirety of Holy Tradition. Does our cherished citation represent the breadth and depth of the Orthodox Faith, or have we wrenched it from the mouths of the saints to construct our own theory? Again, when we approach these writings with humility—to learn and not to immediately teach—it prevents us from abusing them.

The Book of Life

IF WE TRULY WANT TO comprehend the writings of the Holy Fathers, we must engage in the same spiritual quest as they. A modern Orthodox Christian has the advantage of experiencing patterns of Christian life identical to those of the saints in every age, which grants him or her a unique entry into the patristic worldview. Our starting point should be the ascetical life (often called *praktikos*, "the active life"). Any cursory reading of the Fathers reveals how important this was to their understanding of piety. As in antiquity, the Church today prescribes fasting twice a week, and for longer periods throughout the year, including the Great Fast (Lent), Nativity Fast (Advent), Apostles Fast, and Dormition Fast. This practice of disciplining the desires of the body has always been coupled with personal prayer: recitation of written prayers (a prayer rule); simple, repetitive prayers intended to quiet the mind and seek out God's presence (such as the Jesus Prayer); and extemporaneous prayers to address individual needs or challenges. A third pillar of asceticism is charity or "acts of mercy" (in Greek, *eleēmosynē*) which serves to break down a person's ego and teach mercy and selfless love. When undertaken in unison, prayer, fasting, and charity open up a Christian to divine grace and should therefore be considered a prerequisite for reading the Fathers.

Another essential way of imbibing the worldview of the Fathers is by immersing ourselves in the regular services of an Orthodox parish or monastery. Many non-Orthodox scholars commonly miss important themes in patristic texts because they are unfamiliar with the ethos of Orthodox worship. Although the liturgical services of the Orthodox Church—both the daily cycle and the weekly Divine Liturgy—have developed over time, it would be fair to say that if St. John Chrysostom walked into a twenty-first century parish in the United States he would certainly recognize the worship he witnessed. Changes in structure or mode of celebration have not been drastic over the centuries, and almost all the prayers and hymns the Church uses today originated during the Byzantine era. As we traverse the ecclesiastical year, we come upon themes somewhat startling to our contemporaries but commonplace to early Christians, such as the sanctification of creation on the Feast of Theophany, the harrowing of Hades and defeat of death and the devil on the Feast of Pascha, and the glorification of human nature on the Feast of Transfiguration. Liturgical worship draws us into the deep symbolic world of the Church and thereby communicates to us realities we would never have comprehended through study alone.

Another aspect of Christian life that has not changed over time is participation in the Holy Mysteries. These sacramental acts include Baptism and Chrismation, reception of the Eucharist, Confession and remission of sins, and many more. All the saints were initiated into these signs and expressions of God working through His created order (what St. Augustine of Hippo called "a visible form of an invisible grace"[2]). And as many of the Fathers were themselves clergymen—set apart and ordained to administer these Sacraments to the faithful—they possessed a deeper understanding of these rites than the average layperson. Their internalization of the Sacraments is woven throughout their writings, as evidenced by the many references and allusions to them. A modern Orthodox Christian who regularly prepares to receive the Eucharist, or who is married in the Church or has their child baptized in the Church, possesses a special insight into what the Fathers envisioned, something not shared by those who stand aloof from these lifegiving practices.

There is one more important aspect of the Church Fathers' spiritual formation that is incumbent upon the modern Orthodox Christian: study of the Holy Scriptures. Father Georges Florovsky rightly called the entire patristic corpus "the Scripture rightly understood."[3] The saints swam in the fathomless depths of the Law, Psalms, and Prophets as well as the inspired apostolic documents of the New Covenant. Their imagination was molded by the stories, characters, and themes of God's self-disclosure to humankind. For us to apprehend the same scriptural light the Fathers discovered, we must likewise be steeped in these verses. However, we should not approach the Bible as many modern readers do, as merely an account of historical events and interpersonal dramas; rather, we must recognize the numerous recurring types and motifs that unite these individual books into a

---

2   St. Augustine of Hippo, "Letter 138 to Marcellinus," my translation.
3   Georges Florovsky, "The Function of Tradition in the Early Church," *Greek Orthodox Theological Review* 9, no. 2 (1963): 182.

single narrative about salvation (more on this in chapter 4). Once we begin to identify these connections, they will inform how we understand our entire Christian life: how we undertake asceticism, how we interact with the Divine Liturgy, and how we interpret the works of the Fathers. Because Orthodox Christianity is holistic—each part informing the whole and vice versa—we cannot contemplate the Holy Fathers unless we come to know the entire world they themselves experienced and embodied.

Scholarship: The Good, the Bad, and the Ugly

WHEN WE APPROACH THE WRITINGS of the Fathers, dealing with patristic scholarship is unavoidable. First of all, very few readers are adept at translating the original languages such as Greek, Latin, and Syriac; they require an expert to do this for them. But this raises a concern because every translation is automatically an interpretation. No language lines up semantically with another language on a one-to-one basis. Translators must make choices, which in turn affect meaning. Sometimes this is unintentional: A foreign word may have a broad lexical range of meaning and the translator is unsure which English word best fits the original intent of the author. Sometimes this is subconscious: A translator is unaware of biases that influence his English rendering. And sometimes this is intentional: A translator approaches the text with an agenda by which to purposely influence modern readers toward certain conclusions.

Many of the accessible English translations were completed in the nineteenth century by Protestant scholars; and many more were completed in the twentieth century by Roman Catholics. For the most part, these translations are acceptable and convey the gist of the original text; but we must exercise caution. For example, if we notice that the translation contains a plethora of technical theological words associated with other religious confessions, this could be a hint that the scholar either intentionally or unintentionally skewed the translation, which thereby obscures the meaning of the text. But without knowledge of the original language, how can we compensate for this problem?

Ideally, we would want to obtain translations undertaken by competent Orthodox scholars. These would normally be published by reputable Orthodox sources such as a seminary, monastery, or well-known independent publisher. We should also research the academic and religious background of the translator to ensure he or she is qualified to complete such a task. Unfortunately, the number of English translations available from Orthodox publishers remains small, and we will inevitably want to read publications from non-Orthodox publishers if we hope to continually expand our understanding of the Fathers. A good rule of thumb in this regard is to seek out the most recent version of any translation. For all of the negative aspects associated with current academia, one positive development has been the move away from those interdenominational polemics that once colored patristic research. Many translators today remain unaffiliated with any religious confession and thereby lack a specific agenda. However, if our concerns are still not quashed, we may look for Orthodox scholars who have written analyses of the text in question. Although the commentator may not cite the text in its entirety, his or her research may help us to steer clear of false interpretations.

As already mentioned, reading a patristic source in context requires a thorough grasp of the historical, cultural, and theological milieu a given author inhabited. This means we will also need to examine secondary literature written by contemporary writers. We should apply the same criteria just mentioned regarding translations to these secondary sources, preferring Orthodox writers over those of other religions. And just as we seek the consensus of the Fathers, we should work toward establishing a consensus regarding modern scholarship. Academics frequently disagree with one another, but when they concur it is often a sign that their findings are solid.

One of the best ways to begin our own research is to acquire translations from Orthodox publishers that also contain a thorough introduction or commentary on the text. In addition, we should purchase general references on topics like religious history and patristic theology (some of these are included in Appendix C). But one forum we should be highly cautious of is the internet. Although there may be reliable scholars online who provide real information and trustworthy resources, there are many more pseudo-academics and self-proclaimed experts ready to pass off their personal opinions as official dogma. Publishing houses act as gatekeepers, ensuring that the materials they reproduce and sell meet minimum academic standards. The process of peer review (when properly conducted) prevents unqualified individuals from hawking their wares to an unsuspecting public.

Ultimately, we must remember the purpose for which we read the Church Fathers: to deepen our relationship with God. Scholarship is a handmaiden to this endeavor, intended to fill in our comprehension of these texts so that we may better apply them to our lives. We should approach patristic works with the same modus operandi as we do the Scriptures, allowing them to shape our thinking and daily decisions. If our reading does not inspire us to repent, to humble ourselves, and to pursue the gifts of the Holy Spirit then we run the risk of becoming conceited and spiritually deluded (what the Russian saints have called *prelest*). The Fathers are not a club to bludgeon our enemies but a model of holiness offered to a sinful generation. As we begin our journey into their universe, let each of us become a tabula rasa, permitting our Lord to write on us through the words of our beloved ancestors in the Faith.

CHAPTER 3

The Fathers in Context

N OW THAT WE HAVE TOUCHED on some dangers to avoid when reading the Holy Fathers, we can elaborate on a positive method for broaching these important works. In this chapter we will examine some beneficial presuppositions to maintain, how to situate a given author within his historical context, how to determine which texts are more authoritative than others, and how to derive inspiration for application to our own lives.

Philosophical Presuppositions

MODERN SCHOLARS HAVE DEBATED THE question of the relationship between Christianity and Greek philosophy many times. Most famously, German historian and theologian Adolf von Harnack theorized that Christianity had become entirely entangled with the philosophical systems of Plato, Aristotle, and Plotinus during the ante-Nicene and Byzantine periods. He believed the Hellenizing mindset of Gentile converts had subverted the rustic, simple faith of those first Jewish believers. His ideas strongly influenced later researchers and remain a talking point for many historians. Because of this, Greek philosophy has become the linchpin in a history of religion, used to explain any perceived divergence between the faith seen in the New Testament and that of the institutional Church.

This narrative is problematic for a few reasons. First, Greek philosophy had already begun to infiltrate Second Temple Judaism before the coming of Christ. During the Second Temple period, which lasted from the sixth century BC until the temple's destruction in AD 70, the conquests of Alexander the Great brought the Jews under Hellenic domination. This commenced a process of exchange between the Hebrews and Greeks. The sacred books of Israel were translated into Greek, and extra-biblical literature from this period was often written in Greek. Philosophical terminology was even employed to convey Jewish concepts. We find this, first of all, in the Greek Old Testament, especially in the so-called deuterocanonical books like Wisdom of Solomon (for example, 7:22–23 uses the adjective *noetic* to refer to spiritual reality).[1] Outside of the Bible, we find philosophical terms used to describe God in a privative way (describing what He *is not* rather than what He *is*). In texts such as the *Sibylline Oracles*, the *Letter of Aristeas*, and the writings of Philo we find adjectives such as "uncreated" (*agenētos*), "self-sufficient" (*anendeēs, aprosdeēs, anepideēs*), "invisible" (*aoratos*), and "uncircumscribed" (*aperigrafos*).[2] This way of speaking about divinity, made possible by the Greek language, was suitable for describing a God who is entirely transcendent in His essence, even if knowable in and through His activity.

The New Testament did not escape influence by Greek philosophy either. Saint Paul, one of the most versed of the apostles in Hellenic culture, favorably quotes Menander, Epimenides, and Aratos.[3]

---

1   From the Greek word *nous*, meaning "mind."
2   Jean Danielou, *A History of Early Christian Doctrine Before the Council of Nicaea: Gospel Message and Hellenistic Culture* (Darton, Longman & Todd, 1973), 310–16.
3   Robert Jamieson, A. R. Fausset, and David Brown, *Commentary Critical and Explanatory on the Whole Bible* (Logos Research Systems, Inc., 1997).

A latter passage from Acts is of particular interest in that the apostle addresses philosophers of the Areopagus in Athens. Here he borrows heavily from their parlance when he describes God as the one in whom "we live and move and have our being" (Acts 17:28). Like Philo before him, St. Paul likewise utilizes privative language in his epistles to describe divinity in a way that preserves mystery: God's ways are "unsearchable" (*anexeravēta*) and "inscrutable" (*anexenevrētos*);[4] He is "unapproachable" (*aprositos*);[5] and His gifts are "indescribable" (*anekdiēgētō*).[6] With this St. Paul establishes a template for the early Church, thereby sanctioning the appropriation of philosophical terms to convey the teachings of Christianity.

Many of the earliest Church Fathers borrowed terminology from Plato, Aristotle, and the Stoics while simultaneously criticizing the presuppositions and conclusions of these same philosophers. Beginning with St. Justin Martyr, a dialectic between the proper and improper use of philosophy developed.[7] To what extent, the Fathers asked, would it be acceptable to couch the teachings of Christian Faith in terms drawn from pagan speculations? Traditionalists such as St. Irenaeus of Lyon, St. Methodius of Olympus, and St. Theophilus of Antioch would carefully discriminate between right and wrong usage by following in the footsteps of St. Paul: Divine revelation must be the source and foundation of Christian thought, while philosophy would merely provide terminology and a conceptual apparatus with which to properly convey this revelation. These saints avoided adopting any philosophical system whole cloth, never permitting secular thought to trump theology. Instead, they carefully discerned which ideas were helpful, often redefining them for clarification.

---

4   Rom. 11:33; Eph. 3:8.
5   1 Tim. 6:16.
6   2 Cor. 9:15.
7   Danielou, *History of Early Christian Doctrine*, 303–35.

This approach to philosophy could be called eclecticism. Constantine Cavarnos provides us with an apt description of this method:

> The adoption of certain notions and terms from Plato, Aristotle, and other pagan writers [did] not make the Greek Church Fathers adherents of such writers. . . . Although they did use many elements from Plato and Aristotle, they chose those elements that did not contradict revealed teaching, but were in harmony with it and helped express or illustrate its content. In other words, their use of pagan philosophy was not a wholesale, slavish one. It was a very selective or "eclectic" use, which left them quite free to criticize the errors of secular philosophy. Material for this eclecticism was provided for them not only by the writings of Plato and Aristotle, but also by those of the Stoics and other Greek philosophers and, further, by ancient Greek poets, historians, and orators.[8]

Saint Basil the Great, the erudite bishop and theologian from Cappadocia, described this process by analogy in his *Oration to Young Men* when he pointed to the activity of the honeybee.[9] Just as the bee goes from flower to flower taking only what is most beneficial from each, so should the Christian read secular literature with discrimination, gleaning only what is most useful from such writers. This method became the standard and guiding principle for the Fathers.

A basic knowledge of Greek philosophy can be helpful when reading the Church Fathers, particularly for determining where they veer away from secular applications. However, an elaborate education in philosophy is unnecessary. It is often more informative to discover how the Fathers use certain ideas in context, and how the ideas reflect

---

8   Constantine Cavarnos, *The Hellenic-Christian Philosophical Tradition* (Institute for Byzantine and Modern Greek Studies, 1989), 19.

9   "Oration to Young Men," in *St. Basil, the Letters,* trans. Roy J. Deferrari, vol. 1–4 (Harvard University Press, 1961–62), 4:391.

the overarching biblical and theological content. The most important thing to keep in mind when delving into the Fathers is to reject simplistic readings that subsume their outlook into a philosophical one. For example, we may be tempted to view early Christian writers as dualistic because they use imagery such as light and darkness, or flesh versus spirit. The tendency toward dualism in Greek and Persian philosophy was rooted in a worldview that pits the highest, spiritual reality against the lowest, physical reality. As such, the human body would be more akin to evil because it is material, and the soul more akin to goodness because it is immaterial. In such a schema, God represents the top of the hierarchy and must be shielded from direct contact with all those levels of existence beneath Him.

Dualism directly contradicts biblical revelation. The dualist sees the human soul alone as capable of purity while they consider the body vile and unredeemable. It was for this reason that Plato referred to the flesh as a prison for the soul: *sōma sēma*, "the body is a tomb." Salvation in such a system means permanently releasing the soul from the body (a view many contemporary heterodox share). However, this stands in stark contrast to the God of Holy Scripture who created the cosmos to be good and who promises to raise up the body of each person to life on the last day. The biblical account of a fall refers to the introduction of corruption and sin to creation as something external and alien. Salvation therefore means redemption and transformation of both body and soul. When reading the Fathers, we must be careful to interpret any language that seems to denote a dichotomy between material and immaterial as actually describing only that temporary severance of body and soul that sin causes. The saints envisage Christian life as a battle between righteousness and unrighteousness, between life and death, rather than seeing corruption as a design feature of the universe.

Another problem a philosophical mindset creates is the rejection of paradox. As a rule, philosophy—and its offspring: logic, mathematics, and science—is concerned with examining our world in minute detail. A common assumption, one that persists to this day, is that everything will eventually be explained if given enough time. Of course, we all benefit greatly from the work of these other fields. Our modern technologies and way of life would not exist without them. And thanks to the philosophers, with their discovery of logical fallacies in argumentation, we can all seek a more rational discourse when we must sort out academic and social conflicts. But there is also a great hubris in assuming our limited minds can ever comprehend the ineffable mysteries of God. A medieval legend from the life of St. Augustine illustrates this.[10] It was said he encountered a boy on the beach who was filling a seashell with water and then taking it to pour into a hole in the sand. When the saint asked the boy what he was doing he replied, "I am pouring the sea into this hole." Saint Augustine replied, "Well that is impossible," to which the boy responded, "And it is likewise impossible for our finite minds to comprehend the infinite God." The moral of the story is this: Theology possesses an innate intellectual humility concerning God and the universe that philosophy often lacks.

To say that divine revelation is the foundation of Orthodox Christianity is also to assert that theology is in fact greater than philosophy. Whereas the latter can be a handmaiden for exploring our world or theorizing about intangibles such as the mind or eternity, only the former responds to God's self-disclosure. True paradox, or antinomy, happens when we hold two seemingly contradictory realities in tension, in such a way that normal human reasoning would be incapable of grasping. The Creator, who depicts Himself as being beyond all created categories, will not be tamed by His creatures. Hence most of the famous heresies throughout the history of Christianity have been

---

10   Contained in the medieval text *The Golden Legend*, compiled by Jacobus de Voragine.

the result of applying man-made philosophical methods to divinely revealed truths. This is especially true when referring to the two primary dogmas of the Orthodox Church: the Trinity and the Incarnation of the Son of God. For this reason, we must reiterate how vital it is to develop a biblical worldview, assimilating the same sacred texts that formed the Holy Fathers in their own thinking.

There are countless interesting arguments that philosophy makes concerning the world. Many of these are useful for sharpening our perceptions or getting us to think outside of the box. One of the most humorous stories comes from the life of Plato, who once defined a human being as "a featherless biped." To make a point, his philosophical rival Diogenes bought a dead chicken in the market, plucked out all its feathers, and brought it to Plato. As he held it high, Diogenes proclaimed, "Behold, the man!"[11] The tradition of challenging assumptions, pursuing wisdom, and deepening our understanding of human nature is as old as humankind itself, and is likewise an important theme in the biblical wisdom literature. The Holy Fathers, in their own pursuit of wisdom, likewise employed deductive reasoning (syllogisms) and other forms of philosophical analysis to form cogent arguments. In other words, their writings make sense. Even so, they often pointed out that God's logic does not always square with ours. Perhaps this is truer now than in the past, as we are so very disconnected from that enchanted world of premodern Christendom.

As we begin to read the Church Fathers, having reliable reference literature at hand can be very helpful when we face new philosophical terms or ideas. These secondary sources do some of the work for us, making the Fathers more accessible. A basic primer on Greek philosophy that covers the period from the pre-Socratics through Middle Platonism should be sufficient (see Appendix C).

---

11 Diogenes Laertius, "The Cynics: Diogenes," in *Lives of the Eminent Philosophers*, trans. Robert Drew Hicks, vol. 2 (Harvard University Press, 1925), 6.

Theological Presuppositions

MORE IMPORTANT THAN PHILOSOPHICAL INFLUENCES on the Church Fathers are the theological assumptions that undergird their thinking. Of course, we may discover unique questions a given text brings to bear, which reflect the interests and perceived needs of the individual author; and yet we should also be aware of the general conceptual universe these saints inhabited. Their imaginations were molded by the Holy Scriptures and catechism of the Church and polished to perfection by asceticism and liturgical participation. Although the subsequent list here is not exhaustive, it represents some of the key beliefs that define a patristic mindset.

SALVIFIC IMPERATIVE

THE HOLY FATHERS NEVER ENVISIONED theology as a mental game or mere system of ideas. Like the inspired prophets and apostles who penned the Holy Scriptures, they discerned that everything God does is "for the life of the world and for its salvation."[12] At the heart of everything they did, said, and wrote was a concern for others: those within the Church, who needed guidance, and those without, who needed to hear the gospel. Questions like "how many angels can dance on the head of a pin" or "can God create a rock so heavy He can't lift it" are not only ridiculous and nonsensical but also antithetical to the true purpose of patristic theology. The Fathers were concerned with correct doctrine and practice as they saw firsthand how heterodoxy distances a person from God, ultimately leading to rebelliousness, immorality, and schism. The saints

---

12 From the Proskomedia or Prothesis prayers before the Divine Liturgy, with reference to John 6:33.

took their vocations seriously, whether as bishop, presbyter, monastic, or lay theologian.

When we engage the Church Fathers, we should adopt their motivation for writing as our motivation for reading. They erected these markers to point us toward salvation and sanctification, not for selfish and self-satisfying intentions. The best way to avoid this morass is to apply what the Fathers say to ourselves and not to everyone else. Who is that deceitful man that St. John Chrysostom speaks of in his sermon? I am. Who is that prodigal son that St. Cyril of Alexandria refers to in his commentary? I am. A sure sign that we are misreading the text is when we see ourselves as saints and everyone else as sinners. Reading patristic sources requires introspection and self-awareness. Inasmuch as we must interpret the words of the saints, their words must likewise interpret us.

Keeping in mind this salvific imperative helps us to understand why the Fathers were so concerned with precision in theological expression. A false theological premise will necessarily point us toward a false god. If it is possible to construct mental idols—even when formulated from bits and pieces of divine revelation—it is certainly the case that a host of false ideas will lead us away from the true God of Israel. If we believe that the Father, Son, and Holy Spirit are not equally divine, then our apperception of God is mistaken. If we do not believe that the Son of God truly became man, we cannot interact with Jesus Christ as He is. If we think that the Body of Christ is an abstraction rather than a concrete reality, we will stand aloof from the Church. Ideas have consequences. Therefore, a robust theology will always be prudent and explicit in its expression so as not to become a roadblock to the faithful. For this same reason, many of the Fathers (whether eponymous or anonymous) incorporated doctrinal statements into the hymns chanted at services throughout the year. When we attend Matins and Vespers we are inundated with theological truths which shape our thoughts about God and direct us toward salvation.

THE POVERTY OF IDIOM

THE INFINITE GOD WHO REVEALS Himself to human beings cannot be contained or limited by any created conception. Although language itself is a gift from God, our words—and the thoughts that precede them—are products of our finite minds. Contrary to what the Greek philosophers taught, we do not possess a divine spark or piece of divinity in our nature; therefore, we can never perfectly describe our experience of God or fully express the content of our deepest interactions with Him. Speaking of himself in third person, St. Paul explains such a moment in which he was rapt before God:

> I know a man in Christ who fourteen years ago—whether in the body I do not know, or whether out of the body I do not know, God knows— such a one was caught up to the third heaven. And I know such a man—whether in the body or out of the body I do not know, God knows—how he was caught up into Paradise and heard inexpressible words, which it is not lawful for a man to utter. (2 Cor. 12:2–4)

The apostle understood well the poverty of human idiom and why silence should be preferred. His description of the indescribable became a paradigm all the Fathers followed.

Even when a saint offers a description of his or her encounter with God, it is always couched in incredible terms that hardly exhaust the majesty of what they experienced (see Isaiah 6 and Ezekiel 1). The Lord knows that we can only make sense of the world through rational engagement with it, and so we are given patterns and symbols to enable us to venture beyond simplistic meanings and toward the numinous. When we read a patristic text, we must be careful not to gloss over these images when we come across them. A symbol always points beyond itself, revealing something essential. For example, for the Fathers, water is not merely water: It is chaos and destruction, the power of floods and tsunamis, and the abode of monsters; and it is also life and regeneration, rebirth in Christ, and even the Holy Spirit, who pours forth like a fountain from the Father. As St. Nikolai explained in his work *The Universe as Signs and Symbols*, "Unless God reveals to us some of His great mysteries, we cannot get them by force nor theft. . . . Even so, God through innumerable signs and symbols, as through a mirroring of nature, reveals the way we ought to travel in safety and security."[13]

Similar to symbolic language is the use of privative language to describe an experience of God, a concept we have already encountered in our discussion about philosophical presuppositions. In Greek, this is often accomplished by affixing an alpha or *a* in front of a word in the same way we add the un/in/im prefix to English words (e.g., "impossible" or "unknown"). This reminds us that God surpasses our human understanding. Or sometimes the Greek prefix *hyper* is used, which means "above" or "beyond" (*super* in Latin). These linguistic methods facilitate description without circumscription. Theologically, they are part of a larger framework called apophaticism. An apophatic approach is meant to preserve the infinite grandeur and mystery of God and prevent our minds from fashioning conceptual idols. This may be contrasted with cataphaticism: what we can say positively about God. So, for example, if we presume that God is good—based on His revelation to humankind as documented in the Bible and the experience of the saints—we must simultaneously recognize that our perception of the good is limited to what we have personally experienced, or by the highest good we can conceptualize. As finite creatures, we cannot imagine the infinite goodness of a God who transcends every created category. Our response should be: if we are good then God is not God (according

---

13   Nikolai Velimirovich, *The Universe as Symbols & Signs: An Essay on Mysticism in the Eastern Church* (St. Tikhon's Monastery Press, 2010), 82–83.

to our standards); or better yet, God must be beyond any concept of goodness we can conceive of.

As a caveat, apophaticism and cataphaticism are not intellectual endeavors. Vladimir Lossky, a renowned Orthodox theologian of the twentieth century, pointed out in his seminal work *The Mystical Theology of the Eastern Church* that discourse about God is not as easy as contrasting positive and negative language about Him.[14] In fact, it is impossible to know God through language alone. Saint Gregory of Nyssa used the account of Moses on Mount Sinai to help us understand what is at stake. To know the Lord, we must enter into the luminous darkness.[15] We must transcend word and image to stand face-to-face with the living God. Only when we leave behind created concepts are we able to meet God-as-He-is rather than God-as-we-assume-Him-to-be. This is what the Scriptures mean when they speak of knowing God: It is not simply knowing things *about* God, it is knowing God Himself—relationally, intimately. The God who spoke to the Church Fathers is also the God of Abraham, Isaac, and Jacob; each saint entered into a personal relationship with the Lord, a dialogical interaction that was unique to the seer, even if universal in scope.

Those who intended to meet God prepared themselves first so that they could stand in His presence. It is as St. John the Evangelist wrote: "Beloved, now we are children of God; and it has not yet been revealed what we shall be, but we know that when He is revealed, we shall be like Him, for we shall see Him as He is. And everyone who has this hope in Him purifies himself, just as He is pure" (1 John 3:2–3). The Holy Fathers, in purifying their hearts and minds, moved beyond every idol and came to know God through a

---

14   Vladimir Lossky, *The Mystical Theology of the Eastern Church* (SVS Press, 1976), 25–43.

15   See sections 152–169 in St. Gregory of Nyssa, *The Life of Moses*, trans. Abraham Malherbe and Everett Ferguson (Paulist Press, 1978), 91–97.

personal, deifying experience. When reading their works, we must bear in mind that they describe things beyond our comprehension. But if we follow in their footsteps, we will likewise establish a friendship with the immutable and infinite God—and this encounter will be wholly indescribable.

THE UNCREATED-CREATED CHASM

WE ALREADY TOUCHED ON THE fact that God is beyond our human conceptions and we cannot describe Him thoroughly with human language. But the Church Fathers go even further: God is unknowable in His essence. That is to say, we cannot know God in any way similar to how He knows Himself. The word *essence* is derived from Latin *esse* or "to be." This is a translation of the Greek participle for being, *ousia*. This is an apt description for how we describe God in Himself because the Hebrew name Yahweh revealed to Moses in Exodus means "I was / I am / I will be / I do / I make." The divine name was later translated into Greek in the Septuagint as "O Ōn" or "He Who Is" (which is always written in Christ's halo in Orthodox icons). When we speak of God's essence, we are referring to the manner in which He exists rather than a substance He is made of. In order to know how God exists, we would ourselves have to be divine by nature, which is impossible. But why is this so?

One of the tenets of patristic theology is that there is an impassible chasm between the uncreated and created. The Fathers believed that the tri-hypostatic God (Trinity) is the only reality that has always existed: before space, before time, before any cosmological laws, before matter or antimatter, before anything. Besides God, nothing that exists in the cosmos has existed from all eternity; He "made them of things that were not" (2 Macc. 7:28). Thus, every created thing is entirely contingent, existing only because God has willed and continues to will it into existence. As St. Philaret of Moscow wrote, "The creative word is like an adamantine bridge upon which creatures are placed, and they stand under the abyss of the divine infinitude, over the abyss of their own nothingness."[16] This idea helps us to understand how the Fathers approached theology.

When St. Athanasius stood against the heresy of Arianism in the fourth century, he looked to the Bible for evidence to demonstrate that the Son of God stands on the uncreated side of this divide. Although Arius would collect random biblical verses to assert his case that the Son is a creature, St. Athanasius would amass many more passages to prove that the Son is in fact the infinite, timeless Creator. The Nicene Creed summarized these passages by describing the Son of God as the one "by whom all things were made." The Fathers would later employ this same argument to defend the doctrine of the Holy Spirit's divinity stating that He eternally proceeded from the Father. The chasm between uncreated and created is fundamental to understanding God vis-à-vis His world. Our theological reflection should begin with the fact that He is entirely other, surpassing any human cognition.

At the same time, the saints teach us that God is "everywhere present and filling all things." Although He is entirely transcendent, He is simultaneously entirely imminent as He acts in His creation and is close to our hearts. How do the Fathers reconcile this contradiction? An adage that summarizes patristic doctrine states, "God is not place, He is being." In other words, we cannot conceive of God as a thing within a universe of things. He is not a substance or material that somehow overlaps the seen and unseen realms. He can be fully present in the world while being completely distinct from it. He fills

---

16   "Address on the Occasion of the Recovery of the Relics of Patriarch Alexey" (1830) in *The Works of Philaret, Metropolitan of Moscow: Discourses and Speeches: Vol. III* (Moscow, 1877), 436; quoted in Georges Florovsky, "Creation and Creaturehood," in *The Collected Works of Georges Florovsky Vol. III: Creation and Redemption* (Belmont, 1976), 45.

it in a way that is entirely active, not passive. In other words, He is constantly interacting with His creation through His love, grace, and power. This continually creative action is referred to as His uncreated energies, activities, or operations. We should not think of these energies as something separate from God; nor should we envision them as some sort of radiation emitted by God; rather, they are God acting upon, in, or through the cosmos.[17] As such, these activities are also the way we come to know God.

By analogy, we could say this is similar to the way we come to know another human being. We do not, somehow, peer into their being or read their minds; we know them by what they do, by their words, deeds, body language, etc. The Church Fathers understood that we come to know the Persons of the Trinity in the same way we come to know any man, woman, or child: through interaction. The difference, of course, is that God does not act from without, as an external agent, but within. He bridges the uncreated-created chasm by this means, transforming without destroying what is essential to a creature. And by entering into His created order by means of the Incarnation, God intimately unites Himself to our nature, thereby infusing it with His uncreated life. The divine and human natures are never blended, but the latter is changed by the former. Saint Athanasius summarizes this miracle with shocking language: "For He became human that we might be made god."[18] By God's active grace, creatures become "partakers of the divine nature" (2 Pet. 1:4).

THE HYPOSTATIC UNION

SOLOMON ONCE REMARKED, "THERE IS nothing new under the sun" (Eccl. 1:9). And yet there was one unique and earth-shattering

---

17   See chapter 7 on St. Gregory Palamas for more information on this.

18   *On the Incarnation*, 54 [my translation]. The verb translated "made god" may also be rendered "made divine."

event to come, something only prophesied in his day—the Incarnation of the Son of God. The Church Fathers were at pains to ensure that the Church always preserved a proper understanding of this foundational doctrine of Faith. Many heresies have originated from an incorrect answer to the question Jesus asks: "Who do you say that I am?" (Matt. 16:15). Patristic theology defends the astonishing miracle described in the prologue to John's Gospel:

> In the beginning was the Word, and the Word was with God, and the Word was God. He was in the beginning with God. All things were made through Him, and without Him nothing was made that was made. . . . And the Word became flesh and dwelt among us, and we beheld His glory, the glory as of the only begotten of the Father, full of grace and truth. (John 1: 1–3, 14)

As revealed in the Scriptures, Jesus Christ is simultaneously fully God and fully man. This mystery is what St. Cyril of Alexandria dubbed "the hypostatic union."

Before we unpack this term further, it is necessary to go back to his predecessor, St. Gregory the Theologian. In his debate with the heretic Apollinaris, St. Gregory asserted that, "The unassumed is unhealed, but what is united with God is also being saved."[19] Apollinaris taught that the Son of God had indeed become human, but the point of union was the mind (nous). Unlike a normal human being whose mind represents the highest faculty of their immaterial life, Apollinaris asserted that the eternal Word took the place of Jesus' human mind. However, St. Gregory averred that if Jesus Christ did not possess a human mind, then our own human minds are incapable

---

19   Gregory of Nazianzus, "Letters" in *On God and Christ: The Five Theological Orations and Two Letters to Cledonius*, trans. Lionel Wickham and Frederick Williams (SVS Press, 2002), 158.

of being transformed by the Incarnation. To sanctify and raise up human nature, Jesus must be truly consubstantial with it.

Then, in the early fifth century, Nestorius of Constantinople began to teach that the Son of God and Jesus Christ were two distinct Persons (albeit united in some fashion). Following the teaching of St. Gregory, St. Cyril challenged Nestorius on the grounds that only a true union of divinity and humanity—without admixture—could transform and save us. From the moment of His conception in the womb of the Ever-Virgin Mary, the Son of God assumed everything that we consider human, yet without the deleterious effects of corruption brought on by Adam's disobedience. In order to preserve this biblical witness, St. Cyril stated that the focal point of union between human nature and divine nature is the *hypostasis* or "personhood" (*prosōpon*) of the Son: The very same Person who is eternally begotten of the Father also became man, the one whom we call Jesus the Christ. God took on a fully human existence, a physical body enlivened by a noetic soul. Therefore we can never speak of two separate Sons, but only one Lord Jesus Christ, the God-Man, a single subject. Saint Cyril's doctrine was affirmed as apostolic at the Synod of Ephesus (Third Ecumenical Council). And at the subsequent Synod of Chalcedon (Fourth Ecumenical Council), his name and writings were invoked posthumously by the hierarchs gathered to confirm that, in the union of divinity and humanity in Christ, the two natures were unconfused and unchanged but also indivisible and inseparable.[20]

Many contemporary Orthodox scholars have pointed out that the theology of Ephesus and Chalcedon is imprinted on all patristic thought. We cannot comprehend the purpose of the Incarnation unless we think in these terms; and we cannot in turn adequately

---

20 For a detailed account of this, see John McGuckin, *Saint Cyril of Alexandria and the Christological Controversy* (SVS Press, 2004).

describe the mystery of the Church or the Sacraments without reference to an Orthodox view of the Incarnation. Like all the theological presuppositions of the Fathers, the hypostatic union is rooted in a salvific imperative.

THE GOAL OF THEOSIS

ALL THE PRESUPPOSITIONS WE HAVE covered thus far are intertwined in the thought of the Holy Fathers and ultimately point to the *telos* or "goal" for which God has established the world: eternal life. The Fathers taught that salvation is an ongoing process that blossoms over the course of a lifetime and reaches its final conclusion in the age to come. Although they used many different phrases and analogies to describe this movement, we may sum them up with the term *theosis* ("deification").

To broach this idea, we must first underscore that it is, and always will be, impossible for us to become divine by nature. As St. Maximus the Confessor explained, although humans could feasibly have united the various natural divisions in the created order, they could not of their own accord bridge the uncreated-created chasm.[21] Even so, "With men this is impossible, but with God all things are possible" (Matt. 19:26). By the Incarnation, the Lord heals the brokenness of human nature and makes it receptive to eternal life. Salvation, then, is not simply a change in status—from damned to saved, or from condemned to justified—it is a renewal made possible by the presence of God. This work begins with the indwelling of the Holy Spirit in Baptism and Chrismation, then continues through ascetical purification and frequent participation in the Sacraments. Theosis changes everything because God enables us to experience eternity this side of the

---

21 St. Maximus the Confessor, "Ambigua," in *On Difficulties in the Church Fathers,* trans. Maximos Constas, vol. II (Harvard University Press, 2014), 103–21.

judgment, to receive a foretaste of the heavenly banquet. Christian life is about much more than simply holding on to certain doctrines or following a list of rules: It is about fostering an intimate relationship with God in the here and now.

In the writings of the Fathers, theosis is always hidden just beneath the surface. They often describe it borrowing terminology from the philosophers. One writer might emphasize that a Christian should overcome vices and cultivate virtues. However, unlike the pagan Greeks, this is understood as synergy, a cooperation with divine grace rather than a merely human effort. Here the vices are synonymous with sins and virtues synonymous with gifts of the Spirit. Another writer might posit the goal as dispassion (*apatheia*). A passion is an internal tendency a person struggles with (taken from the Latin word for suffering). It is not the transgression itself, or even the associated temptation, but rather a proclivity toward both. In general, the passions represent the disordered spiritual condition of an individual. In resisting sin and following the commandments—once again, in cooperation with divine grace—the believer is set aright, put in order by God and enabled to move beyond the passions. Her faculties are slowly restored and reintegrated and her desires aligned with what God desires.

When a patristic text describes theosis, whether as a theological doctrine or practical method, the reader should be spurred on to adopt this lofty goal as their own. Many Fathers outline steps to achieve this objective, describing intermediate stages such as purification and illumination as stepping stones to deification or sanctification. A certain author may even provide elaborate depictions of what these various states entail. These are not meant to present a systematic technique, as in a modern how-to book, but to inspire the reader to take seriously the spiritual life. The saints pull back the curtain to give us a glimpse of Paradise, both to inspire us to reach higher and to humble us to discourage pride. With this in mind, we can avoid the danger of self-deception as we peer into God's deep mysteries.

Historical Context

FOR SOME, READING ABOUT HISTORY is a great adventure, while it is a tedium for others. Regardless of our personal sentiments, we must engage patristic texts as historical documents if we intend to gain a thorough and honest understanding of them. Before we approach the Holy Fathers, we need to place them within their proper historical milieu, which will require some effort on our part as we slowly formulate a picture of the historical flow of Orthodox Christianity. So before we even begin, we should familiarize ourselves with secondary sources by contemporary historians that help us put everything into perspective. Appendix B presents to us a general timeline, linking major events or eras in the life of the Church with well-known saints from those periods. And under Appendix C you will find recommendations for ecclesiastical histories that will provide a more detailed account of the historical phenomena.

After we acquire a general sense for history, we will be able to examine a specific text. Before we delve into the treasures hidden within, we must first locate the writing and its author within their historical moment. This is extremely important in helping us to understand the intent, writing style, and later reception of a work. For example, if we were to begin reading the epistles of St. Ignatius of Antioch, a review of the historical background would tell us they were written just prior to his death, circa 107. This places him within the next generation after the apostles themselves, at a time when the Church was becoming increasingly populated by Gentiles (Greeks and Romans). Knowing this, we would expect his writing style to be a bridge between the New Testament writings (some of which were completed only a decade prior) and the Christians of the early second century. This was a time of transition, when the ordained clergy (bishops and presbyters), established as immediate successors to the apostles, were struggling to maintain unity, structure, and sound doctrine in the face of both external, state-sponsored persecution and internal heretical pressure from the first Gnostics. Thus we would not expect to find the sort of lengthy, complex theological reflection and debate that characterizes patristic works after the fourth century (after the peace established by St. Constantine the Great).

That being said, we should not assume that the level of theological accuracy in St. Ignatius's letters is lower than that of his spiritual descendants. We do not here posit a theory of doctrinal evolution, as though the Church was not sure what it believed and needed to figure it out over the centuries. Rather, we recognize only a development of terminology, with increasing precision being required over time in order to cut off or prevent heretical meanderings. In understanding the historical milieu of St. Ignatius, although we would not expect to see specific terms like *ousia* and *hypostasis* appear in his explanation of the Trinity—nor even yet the Greek term *triados*—we would still presume he held to the same understanding of divine monarchy as the Cappadocians: There is one God and Father who eternally begets His Son and sends forth His Spirit. With this in mind, we can rightly understand his comments about faithful Christians who resist heresy:

> I have learned that certain people from there have passed your way with evil doctrine, but you did not allow them to sow it among you. You covered up your ears in order to avoid receiving the things being sown by them, because you are stones of a temple, prepared beforehand for the building of God the Father, hoisted up to the heights by the crane of Jesus Christ (which is the cross) using as a rope the Holy

Spirit; your faith is what lifts you up, and love is the way that leads up to God.[22]

Placing this passage within its proper historical context enables us to understand it better: We recognize in it a Trinitarian statement, even if it points to practical application. In responding to the challenges he faced, St. Ignatius left us a testimony to the development of doctrinal language. As subsequent Fathers responded to the problems of their own day, they would build upon the work of those earlier theologians who helped crystallize theological terminology.

Knowing who the Fathers are responding to is also important. In the case of St. Ignatius, we have only a vague sense of who his opponents were, knowing only for certain that they were akin to the later Docetists who denied the reality of the Incarnation. But for a writer like St. Athanasius, we have a firm grasp on the teachings of his adversary Arius and therefore can see why it was necessary for the saint to adopt a non-biblical term like *ousia* in response to heresy. Having a grasp of the heretics' claims not only helps us frame the historical setting but also serves as a caution against making the same mistakes ourselves. However, not every interlocutor the Fathers engaged was a heretic; there were also internecine debates that helped clarify orthodox doctrine. For example, the exchange of letters between St. Cyril of Alexandria and St. John of Antioch gives us great insight into the dispute over the two natures of Jesus Christ. In the course of this dialogue, St. Cyril was able to reach a point of convergence with St. John, recognizing that doctrine can be phrased in various ways by different parties so long as all exponents mean the same thing by their expressions.[23]

The next important thing to understand are various influences upon the particular Father, both the antecedents whose work was

---

22 St. Ignatius of Antioch, "Ephesians," in *The Apostolic Fathers*, 143.
23 McGuckin, *Christological Controversy*, 112–15.

generally disseminated throughout the Church and those specific writers who greatly impacted a certain text. For example, it is obvious that most of the Fathers after the fourth century were strongly influenced by the three Cappadocians. Even those writers who do not directly quote from them utilize their theological approach. However, when we read St. Maximus the Confessor it becomes clear that he owes a great debt to the thought of St. Gregory the Theologian, as he dedicated an entire work called *De Ambigua* to defending and clarifying the writings of his predecessor. Before we broach the works of St. Maximus, a thorough comprehension of St. Gregory is vital to a productive reading.

Not every influence was wholly sound. Following the dictum of St. Cyril, that "not everything a heretic says is necessarily heretical,"[24] many Fathers thought it appropriate to draw from authors the Church considered more questionable. Perhaps the most blatant example is that of Origen. Already by the late third century his writings were being challenged by men such as St. Methodius of Olympus. The tensions surrounding Origen continued to grow in the fourth century as certain monks developed his ideas into a system (later dubbed Origenism). At the same time, many of the greatest thinkers in the history of the Church were strongly influenced by his works. The Cappadocians admired him so much that they collected the best of his writings into *The Philokalia*.[25] Yet they were careful to overlook his errors and cite only those passages that aligned with Orthodoxy. By the fifth century, men such as St. Cyril of Alexandria were still utilizing Origen (particularly in terms of his biblical interpretation), though they were loath to mention him by name. And by the beginning of the seventh century, St. John Climacus

---

24 McGuckin, 183; citing *Letter to Eulogius*.
25 Not to be confused with the later collection of the same name made by St. Nicodemus the Athonite.

would simply refer to him as "the atheist Origen."[26] The question then arises, is it advisable to read authors like Origen? For the non-specialist, it is necessary only to sketch an outline of such influences from reliable secondary sources to discover possible connections in the Holy Fathers. The same applies for all problematic texts: It is ill-advised to pore over such writings and thus become susceptible to heterodox viewpoints. Only with much experience and discernment can the reader make sense of works the Church denounces, and even then only in small quantities.[27]

Placing a given Church Father within his historical milieu also means envisaging the culture he inhabited. As elaborated previously, we may begin by determining what era the saint falls within, and then research what life was like at that time. It is extremely important not to read a text anachronistically, imposing later cultural standards on earlier periods. For example, during the Late Byzantine era, life in the Christian East centered around the great city of Constantinople, the New Rome. The church of Hagia Sophia became the standard for liturgical structure and aesthetics, and the courtly life of Byzantium became the model for the relationship between church and state throughout the Roman Empire. We learn much by studying historical texts from this time, which reflect the society inhabited by those saints. However, imposing this same cultural image onto an early Byzantine author may cause us to misconstrue what their writings say.

Understanding historical realities also helps us to understand periods in which the Church was unduly influenced by problematic

---

26 St. John Climacus, *The Ladder of Divine Ascent* (Holy Transfiguration Monastery, 2001), 65.

27 This may sound a bit heavy-handed and paranoid, but from a pastoral perspective I have witnessed numerous individuals over the years drift away from the Church or from doctrinal Orthodoxy after becoming obsessed with reading heterodox sources.

trends from without. This became acute after the fall of Constantinople in 1453. For the first time in centuries, the Orthodox world lacked a central polis—an organizing principle to look to, a locus and foundation to disseminate proper theological reflection. The lower Balkan peninsula (including what is today Greece, Serbia, and Bulgaria), as well as the whole of Asia Minor (modern Turkey), were subjugated to the Islamic rule of the Ottoman Empire. Orthodox Christian schools were suppressed or closed, and public proclamation of the gospel was forbidden. During this same period, the Roman Catholic Church was entering into a gilded age (a renaissance), followed in due time by an enlightenment that led to the Protestant Reformation. Many Orthodox clergy and scholars traveled to the West to study at great universities, returning to the East with ideas and imagery foreign to the Byzantine ethos. By the seventeenth century, the tsars of the Russian Empire would likewise become enamored by Western Europe, and under ecclesiastical leaders like Peter Moghila, Patriarch of Kiev, Latin textbooks were even adopted in the seminaries.

The Church Fathers of that age wrestled with the task of maintaining an Orthodox theological mindset even while employing a new idiom. In many such cases, foreign influences formed a veneer over traditional expressions of the Faith, making it difficult for contemporary readers to pierce through. Yet we must not ignore or condemn such patristic works, for a few reasons: First, they demonstrate an unbroken link of Orthodox Christianity that has continued even unto our own era, even if clothed in curious garb; second, they reveal the manifold ways in which Orthodox thinkers have faced heresy in different settings, offering us inspiration to face today's concerns; and third, they contextualize the Faith in modes often more recognizable, couched within language more familiar to us. A perfect example of this is the work of St. Theophan the Recluse. His account of the spiritual life is remarkably ancient and modern at the same time, evidence of a mind immersed in Holy Tradition while he remained conversant with his peers. When reading such texts, we must take care to recognize terminology the author may have drawn from strange wells. With diligence, the reader will parse out real meaning from these later Fathers without being tainted by foreign concepts.

Finally, a word must be said about translation. While learning original languages such as Greek, Latin, and Syriac can be invaluable in helping to comprehend the Fathers, this is simply not feasible for the average layperson. At the very least, the reader should try to get a handle on common terms used in a given text. A more advanced method would be to learn how a foreign word appears when written in its original alphabet. One translator might use "spirit" to render the Greek word "nous" (νοῦς), while another may use "mind" or even "intellect." Although closely related, these English words are not identical in meaning and may alter our interpretation. Locating patristic translations with a good footnote apparatus can be helpful in this regard or finding editions with a parallel text in the original language to compare. It is not necessary to master another language for you to make some basic comparisons and locate familiar words to ensure your reading is solid. But it is also important to remember that the Fathers were not always exact or aligned in their usage of terms. One saint's "heart" (*kardia*) might be another saint's nous. Only by paying close attention to the context can we tell the difference.

A Hierarchy of Sources

A COMMON MISTAKE READERS MAKE is to assume that every writing by a canonized saint is of equal weight and value. But this would fail to take into account the fact that the patristic corpus has, by and large, never been redacted and edited into a single collection of canonical texts. In contrast, the canon of Holy Scripture underwent a sifting process that resulted in the Old and New Testaments. A few may quibble over some of the books included in the Old Testament canon, but everyone acknowledges the outcome of a process that took centuries to complete. Regarding the Fathers, the discovery of authentic texts, creation of critical editions, and collation into collections remains an ongoing work of the Church. A few important compilations have been endowed with a certain canonical status within the life of the Church, often referred to as *paterika*. These books are read regularly in monasteries, and even during liturgical services. In addition, certain collections of sermons by St. John Chrysostom and other homilists are used in this way.

Two more types of collections of writings from the Fathers are called *florilegia* and *catenae*. The former are extracts of important patristic passages arranged according to a certain topic. These were often compiled during councils or by a specific author in order to demonstrate the historical authenticity of a particular teaching. The *catenae* (from the Latin term for chain links) are similar collections of patristic passages but are specifically biblical interpretations compiled as endnotes that oftentimes are included with the original biblical text. Translations of florilegia and catenae are ongoing projects that often lack the same exuberance as other scholarly endeavors.

Ecclesial councils eventually endorsed specific patristic treatises and letters, whether in toto or in part. These may be referenced in dogmatic canons or cited in the *Acta* ("minutes"). Such approval elevates the importance of these texts within the patristic corpus. Second in status would be those works that later saints quoted frequently, which gives them a certain canonicity. The critic might dismiss as mere accident that the Church Fathers found it necessary to cite and emphasize particular works by their predecessors and to omit others. Perhaps they only had access to one text and not another? However, the evidence seems to point in the opposite direction, revealing careful deliberation on their part. During their studies they recognized the "mind of Christ" (1 Cor. 2:16) in other writers, and even in individual writings. But as we are not yet so advanced, we can keep in mind the following caveats as we read.

First, many authors wrote over the course of a lifetime, and their views were gradually qualified over time. We may possess works that span a person's career, but they are not necessarily of the same quality. In the modern era this issue has become more acute. Widespread literacy and access to technology has enabled us to preserve writings from a given saint over the course of their lifetime. Yet no one is born a saint, and many modern elders only reached the apex of their spiritual journey late in life. Placing the writings of a saint in chronological order (if possible) can help us detect a gradual progression of thought over decades as he or she grew closer to Christ. It would be nonsensical, however, to pit an earlier text against a later one by the same author. Instead, we should trace a trajectory through time and learn from this development.

Second, some texts were directed to an individual or group and originally meant only for their personal application. Although we may also benefit from reading the text, we would need to appropriately adjust the guidance to apply it to our own situation. For example, monastic manuals like the *Institutes* of St. John Cassian (†435) or *The Discourses* of St. Dorotheus of Gaza (†565) were not originally intended for Christians living in the secular world. It would be impossible (or at the very least, inadvisable) for a married couple with children to live in the same manner as an anchorite in the desert. However, what these books teach us about temptation, the passions, and how to struggle against sin is as true for the layperson as it is for the monk. A nuanced reading of the text converts specialized advice into universally applicable guidance. (The oversight of a wise spiritual father or mother is also extremely important when we tackle such works.) The same approach is true of texts written to clergy and not intended for the laity; or letters written to an individual and not meant for a general audience. We must take caution when gleaning insights for a general audience.

Third, it is simply the case that some authors and some texts have proven to be more invaluable than others and therefore more authoritative. *On the Incarnation* by St. Athanasius has had a greater theological influence than his annual paschal letters; *On the Holy Spirit* by St. Basil has impacted the life of the Church more than most of his personal correspondence; and *On the Unity of Christ* by St. Cyril has been more widely read than his treatise against Julian the Apostate. The sieve of time and theological reflection has elevated certain writings, weaving them throughout the tapestry of Holy Tradition. We should be extremely hesitant to emphasize or create a theological premise from writings that lack such attribution, or ones so recent they have not yet undergone the scrutiny of generations.

Finally, when we cull data to help us make sense of Orthodoxy, we must be cognizant of a hierarchy between literary genres. The Bible is at the core of Holy Tradition, and the Fathers would never contradict what it has revealed. If we come across an apparent contradiction, it is likely we are simply misreading the Fathers. Second, the Nicene-Constantinopolitan Creed and other dogmatic conciliar decrees (such as the Tome of Chalcedon) are inviolable and act as a lens through which we read both the Fathers and the Scriptures. In third place are the important doctrinal treatises and catechisms of the great theologians, particularly those who flourished in the golden age of the Byzantine period. A lively debate could be had as to which category falls in fourth place or whether one of these genres is preeminent. These would include the writings of the Neptic Fathers (ascetical texts), biblical commentaries or homilies, and hymnography. Next would be biographies about the saints and apologetical texts. And last would be the pastoral and administrative canons of councils or individuals (intended for clergy to read, not the laity). It is important not to concoct strange notions by reading in the reverse order. The reappearance of ancient heresies in our day is due in part to taking random citations from a hymn, ascetical text, or early apologetical work and then attempting to reinterpret the entirety of Holy Tradition through this lens.[28]

The Mind of the Fathers

BEFORE WE EXAMINE SPECIFIC GENRES of patristic texts in part 2, let us review what we have already learned. First and foremost, we must remember that the aim of our study is not simply to acquire facts from or about the Holy Fathers but to acquire their mindset. Through their writings we sharpen our theological dexterity and expand our spiritual horizons. Most importantly, we deepen our relationship with God as we meet Him vicariously through the saints' personal experiences. For this reason, we must take seriously the tools the Church offers us if we hope to understand the Fathers. In our ascetical practice—prayer, fasting, and charity—we clear away the weeds from our heart to permit the work of the Holy Spirit to grow. And by participating in communal worship and receiving the Sacraments (particularly the Eucharist) we permit Christ to take root in our souls so that we may bear fruit. As St. Athanasius wrote, "Without a pure mind and a life modeled on the saints, no one can comprehend the words of the saints."[29]

If you are spiritually on the right track, you can begin your reading in earnest. A preliminary study of Church history should be next on

---

28   For example, the "sophiology" of Fr. Sergius Bulgakov was the product of influences he gained from the poetry of philosopher Soloviev and a personal vision he had, coupled with his interpretation of certain medieval Russian icons of the Theotokos dubbed "Holy Wisdom." To this he added his insistence that "Holy Spirit" is feminine in Hebrew (*ruach*). Father Georges Florovsky, while respecting the man, had little respect for this sort of fast and loose version of theology. Sophiology was later condemned at a local council in Paris in 1935. See Alexis Klimoff, "On the Sophiological Controversy of the 1930s," *ROCOR Studies*, March 25, 2017, https://www.rocorstudies .org/2019/09/03/georges-florovsky-and-the-sophiological-controversy/.

29   *On the Incarnation*, trans. John Behr (SVS Press, 2011), 173.

your to-do list so that you can place the patristic texts within their proper context. In addition, it is wise to acquire a few reference texts in advance to aid your reading (see Appendix C). Then, select a few patristic texts to cut your teeth on. Following the recommendations in Appendix D, I recommend you begin with easier texts and advance toward those of greater difficulty. It is also helpful to start in earlier time periods and then advance through the centuries. This will make it easier to detect developments in terminology and imagery, and to make connections with other writers from the same era.

Before you begin a particular text, research who the author is, his time period, and other contextual data. You can often find this in the introduction to a translation, but not always: You may have to track down other resources for this. And get to know the saint you are about to read. Look up his entry in a synaxarion (which contains the lives of the saints); and ask for his intercessions in guiding your study. Finally, as you commence your reading of the text, peruse it once, quickly, to get the gist of the work; and then read it again more slowly, taking notes and examining individual passages in depth. This is a method of close reading and yields more fruit than a cursory or disjointed examination. It is better to read five texts well than twenty-five poorly. And as you read, remember that you are not simply acquiring information but mining precious metals. Apply these nuggets of wisdom to your own life, and let the saints guide you along that same path they once trod.

After advancing through the degrees of difficulty and becoming adept at plumbing the depths of the Fathers, you may want to adopt a broader style of reading. For example, you may read the entire corpus of an individual saint (or at least what is available in languages you understand). When doing this, read the works in the chronological order in which they were written as a way to detect a progression of the saint's thought over time. Another approach would be to read topically: for example, to study all the available works directed against

Arius or all the available commentaries on the Gospel of John. When we are able to hear the multivalent voices of the Church Fathers, each representing an inspired facet of a theme, we begin to hear and appreciate their beautiful harmony.

Now that we have outlined a proper hermeneutic or methodology for reading patristic texts, we will examine literary genres in part 2. Each category of writings will be explicated through specific examples from the Fathers. I recommend reading this second section before tackling texts on your own, as it will enhance your comprehension and make it easier to distinguish the unique aspects of each work.

PART 2

Application

CHAPTER 4

Biblical Exegesis

THE MOST PROLIFIC GENRE OF patristic literature is that
of commentary on the Holy Scriptures. Because the Bible is
the core or foundation of Holy Tradition, it only makes sense that
the Church Fathers spent ample time immersed in the writings of
the prophets and apostles. All authentic Christian doctrine (orthodoxy) and practice (orthopraxy) is based on this divine revelation—
whether explicitly or implicitly. Holy Tradition does not represent
a parallel body of information but rather an apposite extension of
Holy Scripture—it would be best to say Scripture *in* Tradition, not
and. One does not exist outside the other. So to avail ourselves of the
Bible's riches we must probe this dimension of patristic literature and
learn how to interpret the Bible as the Church Fathers do.

The term "exegesis" comes from the Greek term for "interpretation."[1] Closely related to this is the term "hermeneutics," which
denotes the methodology or tools employed in interpreting a text.
One way of envisioning the process of interpretation is to see hermeneutics like a meat grinder and exegesis like the sausage: In goes the
text (seasoned by prayer) and out comes a savory and cogent analysis

---

1   The ancient rabbinical Jewish term for exegesis is *midrash.*

ready to feast upon. The grinder itself consists of theological and philosophical presuppositions, linguistic skills (and lexicons), historical knowledge, reference to previous commentaries, and various methods of reading. The goal of exegesis is always to draw meaning out from Scripture, never to contort it to one's own purposes (known as "eisegesis," as we explored earlier, or "reading into" the text).

The Fathers understood the Bible to be unlike other texts in that there are always two authors working in synergy to produce each verse: God and the human subject. They did not believe that the Holy Spirit possessed the individual, using them merely as a scribe; rather, it was a bona fide act of "in-spiration," the Spirit of Truth guiding the writer and perfecting his gifts as he worked. For this reason there are two primary layers of meaning that comprise the text. The first layer is often referred to as the literal meaning of a passage or book. However, the Greek term used to describe this layer is *historia* and might be better translated as "the narrative." This is an important clarification because many modern readers misunderstand the literal layer to be the factual or historically accurate meaning of a text (as opposed to a more fanciful figurative interpretation). Indeed, the Church Fathers took the narrative at face value, assuming various historical accounts to accurately reflect real events. However, they also considered the poetry of Psalms, the aphorisms of Proverbs, and the parables of Jesus Christ to be narrative—none of which are historical happenings. Simply understood, the narrative is the prima facie, or plain reading of the text, even when it contains complex themes.

The second layer of a text may be broadly dubbed the spiritual meaning. Various terms were used to describe this stratum of a text, but one of the more popular was *anagōgē* (referring to a movement upward). Because the text is inspired, they believed it only natural that a higher meaning remains hidden beneath or within the narrative. Many Fathers pointed to St. Paul's distinction between the letter and spirit of the Law as evidence of this (see Rom. 2:29, 7:6). What constituted the anagogical meaning differed between exegetes. For many, such a reading was rooted in complex, metaphorical or allegorical readings of certain passages. For others, it was rooted in discovering closely linked symbols, a method of reading called typology. We will comment on this approach in more detail.

In the Greco-Roman world, important documents were sealed by dripping melted red wax on the seam of a scroll and then pressing a stamp or signet ring down into it to make an image. (This practice persisted even into the American Colonial period, when wax seals were placed on the flap of an envelope.) The stamper or ring used to create the images was called a *typos*, from the Greek verb *typtein*, meaning to strike something. When struck down into the soft wax the typos would leave a three-dimensional image representing the sender of the document. But for the seal to appear properly in the wax impression, the image on the stamper or ring would need to be its inverse—a photonegative of the final image. So if the original, negative image of the seal on the stamper or ring was called the typos (or "type" in English), then its positive version in the wax was called the antitype (meaning "instead of the type").

Over time, the Greeks began to use the idea of types to describe a way of interpreting a text. Whenever a certain character appeared early in a text, but then was referenced again later in the same text (albeit in a different light), the two images could be connected as type and antitype. The type introduces a theme, and the antitype in some way fulfills or recapitulates the theme. Besides people, types could also be events, places, things, and ideas. The apostles also read the Holy Scriptures in this way, not simply as a method but as a means to uncover real treasures God had hidden in the text. For example, on multiple occasions the Epistles of the New Testament reference Old Testament images and then reveal their fulfillment in Jesus Christ or within the Church. In 1 Corinthians 15:45, St. Paul describes Adam, "the first man," as being fulfilled in Jesus Christ, "the last Adam." In

Romans 5:14 he even calls Adam "a type of Him who was to come" (referring again to Christ). Saint Peter also employs typology, but to connect an Old Testament event to a New Testament sacrament: "There is also an antitype which now saves us—baptism" (1 Pet. 3:20–1). Here the flood in the time of Noah is seen as an image of death and rebirth through water, and the fulfillment or antitype of this image is Baptism in the Church. This apostolic method of reading was taken up by all the Church Fathers, even those who were more reticent about identifying detailed allegories in the Bible.

A word should be said concerning a modern debate surrounding patristic exegesis. Prior to the middle of the twentieth century it was commonplace in historical scholarship to speak firmly of two schools of early biblical interpretation.[2] The broadest version of this narrative contrasted a narrowly literalist Antiochene School— which begins with St. Lucian (†312) (or even Paul of Samosata) and extends through Diodore of Tarsus to St. John Chrysostom, Theodore of Mopsuestia, Nestorius, and St. Theodoret of Cyr (†457)— with a wildly allegorical Alexandrian School—beginning with Philo, extending through Clement and Origen, and reaching its zenith with St. Athanasius, St. Didymus the Blind (†398), and finally St. Cyril. In part, this assessment was based on the writings of the Fathers themselves: Adherents to the Antiochene and Alexandrian schools of interpretation sometimes volleyed harsh critiques of one another's hermeneutic back and forth. But more importantly, such an approach created a means to analyze (and teach students) the history of biblical

---

2   According to Donald Fairbairn, this dichotomy originated in the Reformation itself, when writers such as Jean Calvin extoled the Antiochene exegetes for their "literal" approach and demonized the Alexandrians for their allegories. See "Patristic Exegesis and Theology: The Cart and the Horse," *Westminster Theological Journal* 69 (2009): 3–4. This dichotomy became entrenched and exacerbated by the Hebrew-vs-Greek polemic of writers like Hegel and Harnack.

interpretation and the origin of theological developments of the third through fifth centuries.

However, scholars gradually began to express concerns with the two-schools paradigm. First, it was overly simplistic. For example, in what period and with what exegete does each school originate? We have little surviving exegesis from early figures to justify tracing a clear trajectory over four centuries. Second, there is too much overlap between members of these supposed schools. Saint John Chrysostom occasionally uses allegories or extended metaphors. St. Cyril often quotes the narrative at length and states that it is sufficient on its own. And what of those who do not fit neatly into these categories, like St. Ephrem the Syrian, St. Augustine of Hippo, or the three Cappadocians? Any clear-cut distinction in methodology would be hard to locate.

But there is, perhaps, a greater objection to the two schools theory: academic bias. Many scholars' analyses implied the superiority of the Antiochene School due to its penchant for literal interpretation, which they often took as a precursor to the modern historical-critical method. As scholar Jean Danielou lamented, allegory is taken as "a dangerous principle which transforms biblical typology into literary symbolism."[3] Perhaps such academic arrogance is what eventually prompted a challenge to the prevailing paradigm, which led some to abandon it altogether. A key work heralding such a reassessment was *Discerning the Mystery* by Fr. Andrew Louth. His defense of the anagogical appears in a chapter titled "Return to Allegory": "It is allegory that enables us to discern this pattern [of biblical history], and not only discern it but by means of this pattern restore within ourselves the unity and simplicity lost by the Fall."[4] Fueled by such sentiment,

---

3   Jean Danielou, *The Bible and the Liturgy* (University of Notre Dame Press, 1956), 196.
4   Andrew Louth, *Discerning the Mystery* (Oxford University Press, 1983), 130–31.

recent decades have seen the multiplication of academically honest studies highlighting the complexity and beauty of spiritual interpretation. What actually separates or unites the schools has become clearer, and a more nuanced version of the classification scheme has begun to emerge.

Perhaps the most important takeaway from these academic debates is the realization that patristic exegesis is highly complex and nuanced, regardless of whatever similarities we detect in certain writers. Many who have pored over patristic writings have been surprised to discover that the Fathers often interpreted the same biblical passages in different ways. This is evident not only in exegetes from different regions or eras but even those originating from the same time and place. We may assume the saints would generally agree on the Bible in the same way they ultimately agreed on doctrine, but this would be to misapprehend their hermeneutic. If the text is truly divinely inspired, they reasoned, it would naturally contain multiple overlapping meanings. Of course, many Fathers also placed limitations on how far afield such analysis could go before venturing into heresy, and even corrected the interpretations of other saints. Suffice it to say, this should give us pause before we extract meaning from only one or two patristic biblical commentaries. Additionally, the sum of extant commentaries on any given passage does not equal everything that can ever be said and therefore does not preclude the possibility of new interpretations in the future. What would be entirely inappropriate is any reading that directly contradicts Holy Tradition or summarily dismisses a common patristic interpretation.

Our own exploration of patristic exegesis will be guided by two of the greatest commentators in the history of the Church: St. John Chrysostom and St. Cyril of Alexandria. Their output differed in many ways. Saint John was primarily a homilist, preaching through the Holy Scriptures from the ambo at every liturgical service and concentrating on pastoral themes and practical application within the lives of the faithful. Saint Cyril seems to have completed most of his commentaries at his desk, allowing him time to unpack complex themes and symbols and to address the doctrinal concerns of his age. As an introduction to their genius and spiritual gifts, we will briefly examine their lives and exegetical methodology, and then compare their respective interpretations of the first chapters of Genesis regarding Creation.

St. John Chrysostom

Unpacking an exegete's method and style is a difficult task requiring a telescopic view of their doctrines, influences, challenges, and inspirations. To understand the works of St. John Chrysostom requires us to start with his earliest formation. He began his studies under the famous orator Libanius, from whom he acquired the skills of linguistic analysis and rhetoric (it was for this reason he later received the title *Chrysostom*, meaning "golden mouth"). However, he was soon drawn away from a promising career as a lawyer by his desire to serve Christ, and he received Baptism as an adult in 368. He then studied under the infamous Diodore of Tarsus, whose "two-Sons" theology would later be condemned at the Fifth Ecumenical Council. It should be noted that St. John did not take up this heresy in his own writings, as we shall highlight when we examine his hermeneutic.

Eventually, St. John was drawn to the monastic life and went to live as a hermit in the caves outside of Antioch. In addition to dedicating himself to extreme fasting and prayer, he also set himself to the task of memorizing the biblical texts he brought with him. The success of this work was later demonstrated by his incredible memory for scriptural passages in his sermons. After about two years of ascetical struggle and spiritual study, he was forced to leave his solitude due to medical problems, and he returned to the city and accepted ordination to the diaconate by the hands of St. Meletius in 381. It was during this time that he began to preach in the Golden Church, the great cathedral of Syrian Antioch. Around 386 he was ordained a presbyter. His popularity as a homilist and exegete continued to grow, and he often drew large crowds who would loudly applaud his rhetorical flourishes and down-to-earth advice.

In 397, St. John was secretly nominated by Eutropius the Eunuch to be consecrated the Archbishop of Constantinople, at that time a growing urban hub and new administrative capital of the Roman Empire. He accepted this responsibility and began what would be a short tenure, ending with his banishment in 403. Although the people grew to love St. John and greatly enjoyed his preaching, the imperial court was not pleased with his critique of wealth and power, a criticism he often subtly directed at the royals and aristocracy. He shunned the lavish lifestyle of banquets and delicacies once offered to his episcopal predecessors, preferring the simple fare of a monk, and drew from the coffers of the local church to help the poor, the widows, and the orphans.

Another virtue of St. John's, one that would be leveraged against him, was his impartiality, marked by a measured equanimity. In 400, a local council in Alexandria condemned the ideology of Origenism. Saint Theophilus of Alexandria then began to expel monks from Egyptian monasteries who refused to recant the heresy. The most well-known of these partisans were the Tall Brothers, four towering siblings from the Nitria region named Ammonius, Dioscorus, Eusebius, and Euthymius. They sought refuge in Constantinople, appealing to St. John for vindication. Although not a supporter of the Egyptian heresy, St. John took it upon himself to ensure their defense would be heard, which prompted an angry response from St. Theophilus. In 402, the latter was summoned by the emperor to travel alone to the capital in order to resolve the issue with the Tall Brothers; however, he arrived the following year with dozens of other hierarchs and proceeded to hold his own trial, accusing St. John himself of Origenism and ordering his deposition (known as the Synod of Oak). Although St. John protested the validity of the council, the emperor eventually agreed with its decisions (probably seeing an opportunity to rid himself of the troublesome and ascetical archbishop). Saint John reposed in exile in 407, due to the harsh conditions of the terrain and exhaustion from forced marches. His final words were, "Glory to God for all things!"

Unarguably, the most important works St. John left to the Church are his homilies, which span his entire career: first when he was a presbyter in Antioch and then as a hierarch in Constantinople. He delivered the majority of these as he moved through the texts in sequence, though he also produced various topical and festal homilies to address special occasions. Being trained as a professional orator, St. John was able to preach without a written sermon before him. Stenographers would record his words as he spoke publicly, which he could later edit before the final versions were archived for posterity. Thus his homilies capture for us the experience of his original audience while they were also certified for theological accuracy by the saint himself.

Scholars emphasize St. John's preference for the literal sense of the biblical text, as he avoided elaborate anagogical interpretations in his sermons. As his teacher Diodore wrote, "We far prefer the narrative to allegory."[5] This method focused on determining the hypothesis, or general idea of what a passage is trying to convey, with concentration on linguistical details. A goal of such reading was precision (*akriveia*), marked by attention to minutiae, and often it resulted in lengthy digressions. This served well his inclination to explore the moral implications of the Bible, what scholars call the tropological

---

5   "Fragment 93," quoted in John Behr, *The Case Against Diodore and Theodore* (Oxford University Press, 2011), 35.

reading. However, this also put St. John at a disadvantage when faced with scriptural settings that lacked a narrative he could explicate, such as the Psalms. His love for stories often led him to insert other biblical accounts into whatever pericope he was actually preaching on. Even so, this technique lent itself well to the oral setting of a sermon because it drew in his audience.

Modern scholars have often either criticized or lauded the supposed influence of the heretic Diodore of Tarsus on St. John's exegesis. Although St. John studied under Diodore, little of his former teacher's exegesis has survived to give us a sense of his method. However, St. John's famous (or perhaps infamous) friend and fellow student Theodore of Mopsuestia left behind a significant body of work, which enables us to infer Diodore's influence. One aspect of their hermeneutic that proved problematic—an idea that led both Diodore and Theodore to espouse the two-Sons Christology that Nestorius later adopted—was the division of time into two ages.[6] An analysis of Theodore's exegesis reveals that he envisaged salvation as a tension between this age and a second or coming age that begins when Christ returns. At first glance this sounds entirely orthodox; however, his views were more complex. He considered the first age a time of corruption and sin, of separation from God and parcity of interaction with Him, and the second age an as-yet-unrealized, never-ending stasis of sinlessness and perfection. Contrary to the doctrine of theosis the saints taught, Theodore denied the possibility of a true ontological transformation in Christ. Because the "assumed man" Jesus of Nazareth is already experiencing the coming age, he posited, His disciples may receive a small taste of that future age only through the Sacraments and

---

6   This moniker was given by Rowan Greer in his important work *The Captain of Our Salvation: A Study in the Patristic Exegesis of Hebrews* (Mohr-Siebeck, 1973). The following comments on Theodore are based on Greer's thorough assessment.

the pursuit of moral betterment. When worked out exegetically, his theology led to a rejection of most traditional type/antitype relationships (except those the New Testament specifically referenced) and even many commonly recognized prophecies of the coming Messiah. Primarily, he considered the Old Testament to be self-referential, fulfilling the "contemporary need" of the original audience rather than pointing to a later fulfillment in the Church. None of the Old Testament theophanies of Christ, considered ubiquitous by earlier Christian exegetes such as St. Justin Martyr, find support in Theodore's interpretations.

With Diodore as his first teacher, St. John was exposed to the same hermeneutic as Theodore, and they held some ideas in common. Throughout his commentaries, St. John often takes the text as self-referential rather than as pointing beyond itself to anagogical realities. His emphasis on moral themes and their practical application in daily life also mirrors Theodore's focus on the plain meaning and the idea that "Scripture interprets itself."[7] Yet it seems that St. John Chrysostom found inspiration in others beside his first teacher and thereby avoided following him into heresy. He did not follow Diodore and Theodore in their Christological theories. Never does he mention two Sons or speak of Jesus as the assumed man. Nor does he deny the possibility of real participation in the life of God— attainable here and now, not merely in the age to come. For him, the life of Faith is not just rooted in ethical imitation of Christ and acquisition of virtues, it is transformed by grace.[8] In his interpretation of the transfiguration on Mount Thabor, for example, St. John speaks of the apostles as experiencing the eschatological glory of the Son, even

---

7   *St. John Chrysostom: Commentary on the Psalms*, vol. 1, Psalm 45, trans. Robert Charles Hill (Holy Cross Orthodox Press, 1998), 268.

8   Greer, *Captain of Our Salvation*, 275.

if in a mitigated sense because they were still bound by the corruption of this world.[9]

While it is true that St. John preferred the narrative of the biblical text, it would be incorrect to assume he completely ignored a spiritual reading. For instance, commenting on Psalm 9 he writes, "In some things, you see, it is possible to find a 'fuller sense,' whereas others should be understood only at face value."[10] Here he uses the term *theōria*, implying a higher vision or sight, though with limitations: The spiritual sense must have the literal as its foundation. Occasionally, St. John even engaged in allegorical readings. One example is his interpretation of the Parable of the Prodigal Son in Luke 15:11–32. Although he begins with his standard ethical application of the text, he then interprets the gifts given the son upon his return as symbolic figures. In such instances St. John seems perfectly comfortable transitioning from the narrative to the allegorical sense. The Golden Mouth may prefer the literal sense, but he can also make avail of the spiritual.

Finally, it is important to highlight one more tendency in St. John's exegesis: *synkatavasis*, meaning "condescension" or "consideration." One of the ascendant heresies he defended his flock against was that of Eunomius and his ilk. Their philosophy was a species of Arianism, denying the consubstantiality of the three divine Persons, yet it had a special twist: They theorized that the essence of all things, including God, can be fully known according to the names defining them. As there are three names—Father, Son, and Holy Spirit—Eunomius reasoned that there must be three separate essences or beings, each being fully known according to their respective nomenclature. Saint John penned a treatise against Eunomianism, emphasizing instead the utter unknowability of God's essence. And in his biblical

---

9   Christopher Veniamin, *The Transfiguration of Christ in Greek Patristic Literature* (Mount Thabor Publishing, 2022), 97–120.

10   Hill, *Psalms*, 185.

commentaries, he never misses an opportunity to reinforce the fact that God is transcendent and ineffable, known to us only as much as the infinite one chooses to reveal Himself to our finite minds. In application, this means he frequently elided complicated passages, pointing instead to our inability to comprehend them. At best, he reinforces the great sense of awe we should have in the presence of God; at worst, he avoids the more difficult undertaking of unpacking the text, leaving it to his hearers (or later readers) to speculate on their own. But to be fair to this great saint, most of his exegesis was delivered live in front of a congregation, and the complicated meaning of any given pericope would likely have eluded his audience anyway.

COMMENTARY ON GENESIS

SAINT JOHN CHRYSOSTOM PREACHED FROM the text of Genesis on numerous occasions, and a few of these collections survive. The largest set is composed of sixty-seven sermons he delivered during Lent in Antioch sometime before his transfer to Constantinople. The English translation of these (in three volumes) was completed by the late Robert Charles Hill, an Australian patristics scholar who focused much of his career on the writings of St. John. The first volume, containing Homilies 1—17, also contains a thorough introduction (though, it must be said that Hill's appreciation of St. John was as a gifted preacher and not an exegete, which comes to the surface in his comments on the saint). The textual apparatus (footnotes) is also useful, with biblical cross-references and comments on the original manuscript St. John was reading from. As we unpack the Golden Mouth's exegesis from this collection, we will focus on his understanding of the creation and the fall (Gen. 1—3), which in turn will provide a good comparison to St. Cyril's interpretation of the same passages. We will attempt to move through the homilies in sequence but will occasionally jump around just as he does in his exposition of various themes.

Beginning with "Homily 9," St. John describes the creation of man in the image of God. He first reminds his hearers of what he has said in his previous sermon, that God spoke and created everything out of nothing rather than from "underlying matter."[11] He also mentions that he has already given a definition of "image and likeness," which is, the vocation of regency or stewardship over the cosmos, acting in God's stead.[12] In contrast to a two-ages approach that would likely avoid imposing any Christological interpretation on the biblical account of man's creation, St. John avers that the one saying "Let Us make man in Our image" (Gen. 1:26) is in fact "the Angel of Great Counsel, Wonderful Counselor, Mighty God, Prince of Peace, Father of the age to come, Only-begotten Son of God."[13] Even so, he does not go as far as other commentators in saying that man was created according to the image of Jesus Christ—Himself being "the image of the invisible God" (Col. 1:15); rather, he issues a challenge to Arians and idolators who would see in this imaging a way to transpose human traits onto "the one who has no body." He also adds that the image was given specifically to the male, with the woman being "man's glory" (1 Cor. 11:7), hence designating her supporting role.

After this summary, St. John explains the difference between image and likeness. Here he follows a traditional trope of defining the latter as similitude or the potential to embody God's attributes: "We become like God to the extent of our human power—that is to say, we resemble him in our gentleness and mildness and in regard to virtue, as Christ also says, 'Be like your Father in heaven' (Matt. 5:45)."[14]

---

11 *St. John Chrysostom: Homilies on Genesis 1–17*, trans. Robert C. Hill (Catholic University Press, 1986), 118.
12 Ibid., 107.
13 Ibid., 109.
14 Ibid., 120.

This is accomplished by subjecting irrational desires to the innate reason (logos) given humans, an ability that separates man from the animals he is meant to benevolently command.[15] That humans now fear other creatures is evidence of the fall, he adds; but the ability to domesticate some beasts to assist human endeavors is a sign of God's continual care for us. He concludes "Homily 9" by extolling the beneficence of God for all He has done and exhorting his hearers to respond with continual thanksgiving and "a contrite heart."[16]

"Homily 10" continues St. John's reflection on image and likeness. After a lengthy discourse on the necessity of asceticism, he turns to the phrase "male and female He made them" (Gen. 1:27). The purpose of mentioning man and woman here in parallel, he explains, is "to bestow a blessing on each of them," a blessing expressed in the woman's invitation to share in the man's stewardship of the world. This reflects the saint's general conception of male-female complementarity rooted in vocation, with the latter possessing "the same properties as himself, of equal esteem, in no way inferior to him."[17] But because the biblical text has not yet presented the creation of Eve, St. John states that God addresses His commandments through Adam "to two people, despite the fact the woman is not yet produced."[18] This inference reflects the exegete's penchant for the narrative layer of the text.

Having completed the task of creating the cosmos and placing man in the midst to rule over it, God rests from all His works (Gen. 2:1–3). Pointing to Christ's statement in John 5:17 that the Father is always working, St. John Chrysostom states that God's rest denotes an end to His creating out of nothing, not a cessation from action. Now His work consists of "the maintenance of created things, bestowal of

---

15   Ibid., 121.
16   Ibid., 124–26.
17   Ibid., 197.
18   Ibid., 134.

permanence on them, and governance of them through all time."[19] God continues to act in and through His cosmos—a doctrine reaching its final iteration in the writings of St. Gregory Palamas.

In the second Creation account of Genesis 2, St. John begins with the molding of Adam from dust. Although this is "beyond the limits of human understanding," he does his best to initiate his hearers into this mystery.[20] The reference to dust rather than earth, he states, signifies man's humble origins. Humans share the nature of their physical composition with "the plants and irrational beings," which should be a constant reminder that we are not equal to God.[21] Having personally molded Adam, God then breathes a "vital force" into His creature, bestowing a soul (*psychē* or "life") that possesses the capacity for reason (unlike the animals).[22] Mention of the soul then prompts the saint to digress and focus on the care of the soul and the pursuit of virtue. He picks up his exegetical thread again in "Homily 13," where he contrasts the creation of the cosmos to that of man. While everything else came into being simply by a word ("Let there be . . ."), Adam was "shaped by God's hands," which reveals God's unique and personal concern for man's creation.[23] This inspires the preacher to oppose, on the one hand, any teaching that would equate the inbreathing of the soul with some sort of spark of God, or on the other hand, the creation from dust as reducing human nature to equality with animals. In gifting a rational soul to man, God makes him like the "incorporeal beings," and in creating him from dust He makes him a physical being like the beasts. Thus, St. John describes human nature here as

---

19   Ibid., 140.
20   Ibid., 164.
21   Ibid., 165.
22   Ibid., 166.
23   Ibid., 171.

a microcosm: a unity of the noetic (spiritual) reality and the sensible (physical) reality.

Describing the planting of Paradise (Eden), St. John addresses an unnamed interlocutor who would assert that the garden was in heaven. This, he rejoins, would be "opposed to a literal understanding of the text."[24] Eden was on earth, and the rivers that sprang forth there were actual rivers. After mentioning the two trees in the midst of the garden, he reserves further elaboration on their meaning for "Homily 14," which explores where Genesis cites God's command regarding which fruits man may partake of, and which he may not (the fruit of the Tree of the Knowledge of Good and Evil). God provides every other tree in Paradise for Adam's nourishment as a sign of His solicitude. In return, God asks for obedience to a singular command in order to establish a proper relationship between Creator and creature.[25] After this, God invites Adam to exercise his dominion over the world by leading the animals to him to name. The fact that humans continue to give names to them is "a constant reminder of the esteem which the human being from the outset received from the Lord of all and might attribute responsibility for its removal to the person who by sin put an abrupt end to his authority."[26] In other words, every time we consider the kingship man once held over the world, demonstrated by naming the animals, we also consider the role sin—and Adam—had in removing this authority from us.

In this same homily, St. John takes the making of Eve from Adam literally. The deep sleep God imposes upon Adam precludes an experience of pain while having his rib extracted—something like anesthesia used in modern surgeries—thus preventing him from holding a grudge afterward.[27] God then fashions the rib into a woman, which

---

24   Ibid., 175.
25   Ibid., 187–88.
26   Ibid., 191.
27   Ibid., 199.

the preacher distinguishes from creation ex nihilo, emphasizing his earlier point that man and woman share a common nature. Adam responds by calling Eve "bone of my bones, and flesh of my flesh" (Gen. 2:23). Because Adam was asleep when Eve came into existence, his proclamation shows he was "endowed also with prophetic grace," adding the vocation of prophet to that of king.[28] At this point, St. John addresses the question of whether the couple would fulfill the command to "be fruitful and multiply" (Gen. 1:28). Adam foresaw the expansion of the human race, though this would only occur after the fall. He and his wife were naked and unashamed, living like angels and free from the passions that would lead to intercourse.[29]

The serpent finally makes his appearance in "Homily 16"; however, it was mentioned in passing in "Homily 9," where St. John states he truly appeared in the form of a snake.[30] The motivation to tempt Adam and Eve is "the evil spirit's envy" after he sees the angelic life of humans and compares it to the loss of his own "place among the powers above."[31] The devil seeks to "pluck the human being from God's favor, render him ungrateful and divest him of all those goods provided for him through God's loving kindness." He uses the snake as an instrument through which to deceive Eve, preying on her weaknesses. The serpent pretends to care for her, offering grandeur in exchange for disobedience to God's command. The devil's statement, "Has God indeed said that you shall not eat of every tree of the garden" (Gen. 3:1) is both a twisting of God's words and an accusation of divine malice toward humans.[32] It is as if God wants to deprive his creatures of enjoyment. As soon as Eve answers this query, she begins entertaining temptation, a decision that will lead to her downfall.

---

28 Ibid., 201.
29 Ibid., 202–3.
30 Ibid., 122.
31 Ibid., 208.
32 Ibid., 211.

Saint John skims over Eve's internal monologue that Genesis 3:6 describes and instead jumps to the moment of her transgression: She takes and eats the fruit of the Tree of the Knowledge of Good and Evil, and likewise gives it to her husband. "You put faith in the words of the serpent," the saint laments, "and have been ensnared in such awful deception as to be incapable of any claim to excuse."[33] In so doing, she also betrays her relationship with Adam, conversing with the devil instead of him. As a result, man and woman are "stripped of grace from above" and experience nakedness and shame instead.[34] At the close of the sermon, St. John reveals where the tree received its name: It was not because it bestowed knowledge of good and evil, for this was already given by God, but because it would become the experience of good and evil either through obedience or disobedience.[35] This prompts him to consider a typological relationship between the tree in Paradise and the tree Christ was nailed to:

> The former tree brought death, death entering the scene after the fall, whereas the latter endowed us with immortality; one drove us from Paradise, the other leads us up to heaven; the former rendered Adam liable to such a terrible penalty for one transgression, whereas the latter freed us from the countless burdens of our sins and restored us confidence in the Lord's sight.[36]

The last sermon in the first volume of St. John's *Homilies on Genesis* focuses on the Lord's appearance in the garden and subsequent judgment of Adam and Eve. Here he takes a moment to once more dismiss any crass anthropomorphism that implies that God has a body, that

---

33 Ibid., 214.
34 Ibid., 216.
35 Ibid., 220.
36 Ibid., 221.

He literally "strolled in the garden."[37] (This differs from other Fathers who put Christ Himself in Paradise speaking with the couple.) They hide in the bushes, not because they perceive God to be angry, but because their own consciences convict them.[38] The Lord finds them there and proceeds to dialogue with them, condescending in love and gentleness in order to instruct them.[39] But Adam does not respond in kind and instead blames Eve for his sin, and even blames God for creating her in the first place. Saint John puts into the mouth of God a rebuttal, "You are head of your wife, and she has been created for your sake; but you have inverted the proper order."[40] When God turns to Eve, she likewise passes on the blame, claiming the serpent compelled her to sin. God does not address the serpent, however, but simply judges him. For St. John, this means the actual reptile who acted as Satan's instrument is likewise judged on earth and sentenced to "unquenchable fire."[41]

Genesis 3:15, which describes the enmity between the devil and the Seed of the woman, was interpreted as a prophecy of the coming Christ as early as St. Irenaeus of Lyon; yet St. John overlooks any typology here. Rather, he turns his attention to the curses God pronounces against Adam and Eve. These are meant to restrain and correct humans, teaching them to avoid sin and remember God.[42] In addition, the fall alters the order of male and female, which shifts from a relationship of equality to one of subjection. And what of the fact that they did not die on that day? Saint John explains that God's sentence is merely the introduction of death to their human nature, not an immediate adjudication.[43]

---

37 Ibid., 223.
38 Ibid., 224.
39 Ibid., 228–29.
40 Ibid., 231.
41 Ibid., 235.
42 Ibid., 238–42.
43 Ibid., 244–45.

The last comments St. John makes concerning Adam and Eve before he moves on to the story of Cain and Abel are recorded in "Homily 18" (found in the second volume of Hill's translation of *Homilies on Genesis*). Here he remarks on the "garments of skin" God gives the couple after their fall. Their previous "splendid vesture" is stripped, and with it their protection from bodily needs; but in His kindness, God clothes them to cover their shame.[44] Even so, these new garments are those "usually worn by slaves," thus designating the change in their stature and acting as a "constant reminder of their disobedience." Saint John then concludes this inquiry into the Fall by giving the reason why God expelled man and woman from Paradise. Had they seized upon the fruit of the Tree of Life, they would be crystallized in a state of sin. They would "go on sinning forever," and repentance would be impossible.[45] Again, the saint sees in this divine decision an act of condescension and care for human beings, a reflection of all God does for His creatures.

In examining these homilies of St. John Chrysostom, we now have a good foundation for approaching the rest of his works. Although not everything he has left us is a sermon, his entire output shares a certain rhetorical style and pastoral intention. Once we have become attuned to his use of language, common tropes, and theological approach, we can apply this to reading further in his corpus.

St. Cyril of Alexandria

UNLIKE ST. JOHN CHRYSOSTOM, ST. Cyril was groomed to be a clergyman from an early age. The nephew of St. Theophilus (who was archbishop and pope of Alexandria from 384–412), St. Cyril would have received the best education in grammar and rhetoric. While

---

44   *St. John Chrysostom: Homilies on Genesis 8–45*, trans. Robert C. Hill (Catholic University Press, 1990), 5.
45   Ibid., 8.

there is no evidence that he was eventually initiated into the monastic life, later biographers preserve the tradition that he was mentored for a time by a certain Serapion the Wise, which may refer to either St. Serapion of Thmuis or St. Serapion the Great. Such contact would explain St. Cyril's emphasis on ascetical practice in his writings.

Ironically, the first clear chronological note we have for St. Cyril is his attendance at the Synod of Oak where he witnessed the deposition of St. John Chrysostom. Although St. Cyril was only a tonsured reader at that time, St. Theophilus likely invited him to observe the proceedings in order to prepare his nephew to succeed him, hence giving the young man an education in the intrigues of political maneuvering. Saint Cyril would later be consecrated Archbishop of Alexandria in 412, after the death of his uncle. Unfortunately, his early episcopacy was marred by political controversies. The two most notorious incidents were the expulsion of Jews from Alexandria in 414 and the murder of Hypatia the philosopher in 415. However, it is difficult to ascertain to what extent he incited either incident, as testimony for both comes from accounts his adversaries wrote.

After 415, it seems St. Cyril remained aloof from controversy until 428, when he became aware that Archbishop Nestorius of Constantinople had been preaching a novel Christology, one in which the eternal Son of God was believed to have formed a "union of good will" with the man Jesus of Nazareth. Saint Cyril rightly understood this two-Sons concept to be an afront to Holy Tradition, the Bible, and the Nicene Creed. His challenge to Nestorius would lead to the Third Ecumenical Council in Ephesus in 431. There, St. Cyril's hypostatic union, emphasizing a single subjectivity of the one Lord Jesus Christ, would prevail, and Nestorius would be deposed for refusing to recant his teachings. In his final years, St. Cyril would continue to communicate with other bishops who were uncomfortable with some of his sharper theological statements, seeking rapprochement and commonality with those he believed agreed with him in principle if not in terminology.

Unlike his episcopal predecessors in Alexandria, Ss. Athanasius and Theophilus, St. Cyril left us a large corpus of exegesis covering much of the Bible, thereby enabling scholars to thoroughly probe his scriptural mind. Following the example of Origen and St. Didymus, he seemed to work systematically through the Bible starting with Genesis, giving much of his attention to the Pentateuch and Prophets (revealing his predilection for the Old Testament). Sometime before 428, St. Cyril made it to the Gospel of John. It is only after this time that his exegetical output decreased, as he began to turn his attention to the Nestorian conflict.[46] With such a large well to draw from, it is surprising that scholars have not focused more on St. Cyril's biblical commentaries. This is due in part to a bias that has persisted in historical and theological circles. Historians continue to depict Cyril as a ruthless and cunning political despot who exploited various crises both for personal gain and to protect the preeminence of his urban see. Theologians often attack him for misunderstanding Nestorius, and for imposing a Christological model on the Church that is effectively Monophysite. And biblical scholars accuse him of abusing the text with wild allegorism. In addition, many have dismissed his exegesis as tedious and trite, even if they fail to provide any firm evidence to support such claims.

Despite the controversy surrounding him, the Orthodox Church considers St. Cyril to be one of the great doctors of our Faith. Hence, we should reject such accusations out of hand. Commenting on St. Cyril's motivation for exegesis, scholar Alexander Kerrigan points to the saint's immense love for the Bible. He writes, "The numerous quotations, the frequent reminiscences, his very style, show

---

46 His work on the Gospel of Luke, likely delivered as homilies, is an exception, dated to sometime after the Nestorian controversy began.

the extent to which he reflected on and relished Holy Writ."[47] Saint Cyril's mind was like an encyclopedia of biblical passages, which he seemingly materialized at will. In his writings, he quickly and effortlessly bounds from verse to verse across the canon of Scripture, making connections and culling typological inferences as he goes. His knowledge of the canon in toto should dissuade us from considering his commentaries as mere eisegesis or simplistic proof-texting. Saint Cyril perceived the original context but pushed beyond it in forging a vivid intertextualism that was bolstered by extra-biblical material, including geography, historiography, and Jewish traditions.[48] Underlying his interpretations are his solid theological presuppositions, which are firmly rooted in Orthodoxy (of a decidedly Athanasian bent).

Saint Cyril believed that the anagogical meaning did not negate the narrative layer. The *skopos*, or whole meaning of the biblical text, was to be found in the *historia* as well. The narrative speaks of "the things of this earth" and denotes the outer layer or coarse exterior of the Scriptures.[49] Similar to St. John Chrysostom, much of St. Cyril's literal commentary is merely a summary or paraphrase of events in the text. Interestingly, he also included certain forms of figurative and poetic language in this category, including riddles, paradigms, parables, metaphor, simile, personification, innuendo, and hyperbole. In his view, each literary device presents a historical fact, which afterward may lead to an anagogical reading.

Although St. Cyril bestowed greater respect to the literal sense than Origen or St. Didymus did previously, he remained firmly an Alexandrian in his preference for the spiritual sense. While the narrative may have value (especially for the average reader),

---

47 Alexander Kerrigan, *St Cyril of Alexandria: Interpreter of the Old Testament* (Pontifical Biblical Inst., 1962), 201.
48 Ibid., 94.
49 Ibid., 45.

and certainly conveys a true account of things that were, spiritual meaning constitutes the aim of exegesis. The plain meanings of the words become truly valued or necessary when they point to this higher sense. He finds support for his understanding in the Pauline expression of types and shadows (see Col 2:16–17; Heb 10:1), by which he also establishes a general rule concerning the relationship between the Old and New Testaments: "The Law was a type and shadow, the form of religion that brings forth in childbirth, as it were, the beauty of the truth which is hidden inside."[50] Through a spiritual reading of the Bible, St. Cyril brings to the surface its harmony, hence preserving the overarching narrative trajectory of the canonical text.[51] Although he varies the terms he uses to describe his anagogical method, his favorite is *theōria*, a term he uses in a different way than St. John Chrysostom. The Alexandrian understands this as the underlying sense of all the Holy Scriptures, ever accessible beyond the plain meaning and always the primary goal of reading.

GLAPHYRA ON THE PENTATEUCH

A GOOD PLACE TO BEGIN examining St. Cyril's exegesis is with his first major work, *Glaphyra on the Pentateuch*, meaning "elegant comments" on the first five books of the Bible (the Torah or Law). This commentary, which he composed from his desk rather than preached from a pulpit, was meant to be a companion to his *Worship in Spirit and Truth*, a more systematic theological volume that traces the arc of salvation through the Bible and answers the question about the relationship of the Old Testament to the New. In *Glaphyra*, St. Cyril turns his attention to the specific ways in which the mystery of Christ

---

50   Ibid., 136.
51   Ibid., 134–36.

can be found in the writings of the patriarchs and prophets. This already marks a distinction between his interpretative method and the more historically contextualized style of St. John Chrysostom. As we will see, these two saints approach the text in somewhat different ways, although there remains overlap (and there is evidence that St. Cyril may have also read St. John's works).

The first English translation of *Glaphyra* was published only in 2018, completed by Nicholas Lunn, a translator and professor at Spurgeon's College in London. Lunn provides a thorough introduction, including a short (and fair) biography of St. Cyril, a summary of the exegete's hermeneutic, and an exploration of various theological themes within the commentary itself. The translator also provides a solid textual apparatus, with references and brief explanatory notes throughout. The section of *Glaphyra* that contains St. Cyril's account of the Creation and the Fall appears in volume 1 of Lunn's translation. It's a rather terse explanation that takes up less than thirteen pages of the publication. In part, this is because St. Cyril alludes to the companion work, *On Worship in Spirit and Truth*, stating, "We have deliberately omitted the topics covered there from the present work and have included what was left unexamined."[52] This other work is a brilliant exposition on the Faith; but since there is presently no English translation of it available, we will concentrate here only on what St. Cyril says in *Glaphyra*.

Saint Cyril begins with an explanation of Creation quite similar to what we find in St. John Chrysostom's writings. First, he affirms that all things were created through the Son, who was always with the Father. Second, he notes that the mechanics of this incredible act are beyond human comprehension and should simply inspire awe: "For if one wishes to inquire into these things, there is no doubt that he

---

52   *St. Cyril of Alexandria: Glaphyra on the Pentateuch, Volume 1: Genesis*, trans. Nicholas P. Lunn (Catholic University Press, 2022), 52.

will be completely lacking in mental ability, in contrast to that which God is perceived to have."[53] This is the same idea of God's condescension or consideration (*synkatavasis*) that his Antiochene predecessor frequently referenced. Then, after briefly describing God creating and fashioning the cosmos over six days, St. Cyril makes clear that all things were brought into being for the purpose of the creature fashioned to live within this world: "It was essential, therefore, that a rational creature be formed upon the earth, where those things that appeared earlier serve for his enjoyment, and are seen to have been made for his benefit."[54]

Turning to the act of man's creation, St. Cyril points out that, whereas everything else came into existence by one word, in regard to man the Lord "honored the making of this masterpiece with his own deliberation and personal involvement."[55] God sculpted Adam from the soil and made him to reflect "the rationality of his own nature." But where St. Cyril diverges from St. John becomes clear in his interpretation of the inbreathing. God "immediately implanted within him an immortal, life-giving Spirit." In other words, God did not simply animate man with the soul or vital force but with His own Holy Spirit, which at first prevented human nature from experiencing death. This is similar to what other Fathers have posited, as they often described this vesture of the Spirit as a garment that man loses in the Fall (hence Adam and Eve's nakedness after their transgression).

After this inbreathing, God gives man dominion over the cosmos, showing he is "the image of the highest glory, and the representation of divine authority on earth."[56] But at the same time, God thought it "fitting that man should live fearfully" by being "obedient to the laws of nature." Here St. Cyril implies that human hubris should

---

53   Ibid., 54.
54   Ibid., 55.
55   Ibid., 56.
56   Ibid., 56.

be checked by humility. Adam was "to understand clearly that God held a position over him as his King and Lord." To inculcate such obedience, "God immediately issued a law and accompanied it with the threat of punishment should it be transgressed." By this he refers to the prohibition to eat from the Tree of the Knowledge of Good and Evil. Then, Saint Cyril merely summarizes the creation of Eve from Adam's rib, as he also does with the rebellious act of snatching the forbidden fruit and the pair's becoming subject to corruption and death.[57]

So far, the Alexandrian has not exhibited any of the wild allegorism he is accused of but has provided a rather literal explanation of the biblical text. At this point in his commentary, he begins to wax theological. First, he asks rhetorically if it would have been better that God not create human beings, knowing they would eventually fall. This question of theodicy is similar to that of St. Athanasius in his famous work *On the Incarnation*. In answering this concern, St. Cyril shifts the emphasis away from God's justice and focuses on humanity's freedom, and therefore their culpability. Even so, he opines, God "foresaw some greater good."[58] Not only could human nature be cleansed of corruption and receive the "good things that were there in the beginning," it could experience a better state because the Son would come in human form. The story of redemption, St. Cyril asserts, was always Plan A. In support of this he quotes St. Paul:

> So do not be ashamed of giving testimony to our Lord or of me his prisoner, but join with me in suffering for the gospel, relying on the power of God, who saved us and called us with a holy calling, not according to our works, but according to his own purpose and the grace which was given us in Christ Jesus before all ages, and that has

---

57   Ibid., 57.
58   Ibid., 60.

been revealed in the last ages by the appearing of our Savior Jesus Christ. (2 Tim. 1:8–10 [translation mine])

The Holy Spirit, through the Old Testament, "testifies unambiguously to the antiquity of salvation through Christ."[59] Therefore the righteousness of God cannot be impugned simply because some people would reject the possibility of being saved in Christ.

When he defines the effects of the fall on human nature, St. Cyril begins with a "charge of carelessness" that resulted in mortality; but he does not here describe a sort of culpability or guilt legally imputed to later generations. While he does write that "the punishment passed upon all men," he adds, "this condition [was] coming forth just as things grow out of a root."[60] For St. Cyril, punishment here is directly connected to death, the latter being the resulting consequence of corruption infecting human nature. He cites Romans 5:14 in support of this idea: "Nevertheless death reigned from Adam to Moses, even over those who had not sinned according to the likeness of the transgression of Adam, who is a type of Him who was to come." Every descendent inherits the corrupted state of Adam, even though they do not share in his exact sin. But the good news is that this punishment was not to be a permanent state, since before man was even made, God "made prior provision for his own creatures, and prepared for us a second root, as it were, or a race that would raise us back up to our former incorruption." As the saint said earlier in his commentary, the plan for salvation was always recapitulation in Jesus Christ,[61] and this imagery is not simply metaphorical, but ontological. Because the Son of God is life itself, in uniting Himself to human nature He is able to "transform it into life."[62] This is the clear lan-

---

59   Ibid., 61.
60   Ibid., 62.
61   Ibid., 53; cf. Eph. 1:9–10.
62   Ibid., 63.

guage of theosis expressed also in earlier writers like Ss. Athanasius and Irenaeus. Citing 2 Peter 1:4, St. Cyril adds that the indwelling of the Holy Spirit makes Christians "partakers of the divine nature."[63] Interestingly, he then cites Romans 5:18, directly connecting deification to justification.

Wrapping up this section of *Glaphyra* before moving on to Genesis 4, St. Cyril teases out the typology between the first and second Man by comparing the oneness of flesh Adam and Eve shared to the unity of Christ and His Church. The former were coupled by physical intercourse, while the latter are conjoined by the Spirit. Similar ideas appear throughout the commentary on the Pentateuch, revealing the saint's penchant for bringing together the historical work of Christ—as demonstrated across the scope of Holy Scripture through interwoven types and allegories—with the ongoing work of the Church in this current age.

In comparison to the homilies of St. John Chrysostom, St. Cyril spends more time exploring theological themes. However, clear similarities remain between their output: Both tend to paraphrase the narrative at length, never challenging its validity along the way; both support their interpretations with numerous quotations of other biblical verses; and both rely on traditional theological tropes to undergird their comments. Where they differ is that St. Cyril is more ready to make Christological connections across the entire canon of the Bible. And what we have not seen in the section we reviewed, but can be witnessed elsewhere in *Glaphyra*, are the sort of elaborate allegories often disdained by the Antiochene exegetes. Side by side, these two saints represent slightly different methodologies; yet they remain entirely Orthodox in their overall product.

---

63   Ibid., 64.

CHAPTER 5

Letters

I T IS SOMETIMES SAID THAT letter writing is a lost art. The ability to effectively communicate our thoughts in writing, using universal conventions such as salutations and closures, was once a hallmark of civilized society, now replaced by the expediency of emails, texts, and instant messaging. For the Church Fathers, epistolary practice was a necessity, a means to disseminate theological and practical information both to individuals and large audiences. This should come as no surprise as letters comprise a vast majority of the New Testament. The apostles understood the importance of clarifying matters in writing, which left a testimony for the original reader (or hearer) as well as a witness to later generations.

It is possible to divide patristic letters into two main categories: encyclicals and private correspondence. An encyclical is a document that is meant to be circulated between numerous parties. Due to the great amount of time and money expended in creating a letter in antiquity, originals were often passed from one location to another. Recipients at one location were permitted to make a copy of their own for posterity (which often meant hiring a scribe to undertake the task) before sending the letter on to its next destination. Sometimes multiple originals were produced and sent to several locations to be read aloud to gathered crowds. For example, a letter from a bishop might be read at local parishes at the end of a Divine Liturgy. The purpose of encyclicals was always to inform large numbers of people rather than individuals.

The earliest encyclicals in Christian history are the Epistles in the New Testament. Written by an apostle or group of apostles, these provide a model for the letters found in the Apostolic Fathers of the second century. The earliest of these are *Second Clement* (circa 95) and the seven letters St. Ignatius of Antioch composed right before his martyrdom in 107. As the Church began to organize itself around important episcopal sees—later dubbed "patriarchates"—the practice of sending encyclicals to other churches increased. These letters were a means of codifying regional practice, informing bishops and presbyters of news within the wider Christian world, and condemning heresies and problematic practices that may have been spreading throughout the area. They were official representations of the mind of their senior hierarchs, who often found it impossible to travel such long distances in an era before planes, trains, and automobiles.

Private correspondence, on the other hand, was directed to specific people, or sometimes a few people together. Some of these letters were considered highly confidential, particularly when they contained delicate matters such as affairs of the state or internal governance of the Church. They would have been sealed with wax, only to be opened by the intended recipient. But just as often, private letters were also expected to be read by others, at least in due time. Many writers even had a copy of the original made before sending and compiled them into collections for later reference. Through such documents we gain a deeper appreciation of the authors and their relationships with others. As we compare samples from both categories of letters, we will discover the breadth of human communication that could be captured by this ancient convention.

St. Athanasius the Great

A WONDERFUL EXAMPLE OF ENCYCLICAL writing comes to us from St. Athanasius the Great. He inherited a practice stemming back to at least St. Dionysius of Alexandria (†264) in which the Egyptian patriarch would issue an encyclical before the start of the Great Fast (Lent) each year. In his capacity as pope (a title the Alexandrian patriarch always shared with the hierarchs of Rome), St. Athanasius was the nexus around which the northeast African Church organized itself. Before exploring some of his encyclicals, we will provide a sketch of his life.

Saint Athanasius was born at the end of the third century and reposed in 373. Saint Alexander, Pope of Alexandria from 313–326, appointed him his secretary, perhaps due to his education and oratory skills. His talents were soon showcased in the publication of his two apologetic treatises, *Contra Gentes* (*Against the Heathens*) and *De Incarnatione* (*On the Incarnation*), written before 319, when the Arian controversy first erupted. In 325, St. Athanasius—now ordained a deacon—accompanied St. Alexander to Nicaea for the First Ecumenical Council. He would have been almost thirty years old at that time. With the death of his beloved mentor the year after, he would then be elected (despite his objections) to succeed St. Alexander as Pope and Patriarch of Alexandria. His tenure would last until his death but would be a turbulent time.

During his episcopacy, the supporters of Arius, who refused to accept that the Son of God is of one nature with the Father, continually persecuted St. Athanasius. Hierarchs such as Meletius of Lycopolis and Eusebius of Nicomedia curried the favor of emperors and succeeded in having him exiled on five different occasions, each period concluding with the saint's triumphal return. He was so maligned by the heretics that he once quipped to one of his attackers,

"Is the world against Athanasius? So be it. Then Athanasius is against the world!"[1]

Despite this constant barrage of antagonism, St. Athanasius succeeded in leaving behind a substantial corpus of writings. In addition to his two early works already mentioned and his many encyclicals and personal letters, he also wrote the popular *Life of Anthony* about his spiritual mentor and friend St. Anthony the Great; two works on the Arians, *History of the Arians* and *Against the Arians*; and a *Commentary on the Psalms*. His legacy looms large over the Church, inspiring every Orthodox theologian and clergyman after him.

Many of the annual encyclicals of St. Athanasius were compiled and translated during the late nineteenth century and published in the famous *Nicene and Post-Nicene Fathers* collection edited by Philip Schaff and Henry Wace. However, a new translation has recently been published titled *The Festal Letters of Athanasius of Alexandria*, translated and annotated by David Brakke and David Gwynn.[2] They provide several tools for the reader and give a solid contextualization of the source material. They begin with a brief biography of the saint, an important feature to aid in connecting his letters to various periods of his career. A second chapter examines the documents themselves, including their transmission, dating, and content. The encyclicals are divided into five sections: "The Early Years" (328–335); "Between East and West" (335–346); "The Golden Decade" (346–356); "From Desert Exile to Church Father" (356–373); and "The Canon of Scripture" (367), separated out due to its special status within ecclesiastical history. The editors also add an index of the encyclicals, a translation of the *Historia Acephala*

---

1 Henry Coray, *Against the World: The Odyssey of Athanasius* (Inheritance Publications, 1994), 38–39.
2 *The Festal Letters of Athanasius of Alexandria, with the Festal Index and the Historia Acephala*, trans. David Brakke and David M. Gwynn (Liverpool University Press, 2022).

("The Untitled History of Athanasius"), and indices including a historical chronology, list of important calendar dates referenced in the letters, maps, a glossary, and other items. When we delve into the translation, we find numerous footnotes explaining ideas within the letters or providing references. Taken all together, this volume represents a gold standard for patristic texts, giving the reader the tools necessary to enter into the milieu and mind of a Father of the Church. We will briefly examine one letter from each of the four stanzas of St. Athanasius's life.

The first surviving letter in this collection is dated to 329, just four years after the Council of Nicaea. Saint Athanasius had been consecrated Pope and Archbishop of Alexandria the previous year, and this was his first opportunity to write to all the clergy of Egypt prior to Lent. He begins by pointing out the primary purpose of his letter—to offer instructions on the coming fast and concluding feast of Pascha—but then he immediately offers his readers a theological reflection on the nature of time:

> Again, my beloved, the time summons us to keep the feast. Again, "the sun of righteousness" (Mal. 4:2), causing his divine rays to dawn upon us, announces beforehand the time of the feast, during which in obedience to him we ought to celebrate it, so that, when the time has passed by, gladness will not pass us by. For it is one of the most necessary things and (one of) the practices of virtue to discern the time, just as the blessed Paul, when instructing his disciple, teaches him to discern the time, saying, "Be persistent in season and out of season" (2 Tim. 4:2), so that, by discerning both, he might perform those things that befit the time and escape the accusation of being "out of season."[3]

---

3   Ibid., 47.

Rather than simply saying, "the fast is coming," St. Athanasius employs poetic language as he encourages his readers to redeem the time God has allotted to them. We also detect a subtle wordplay in his quote from Malachi, a verse traditionally taken to be a prophecy of the Messiah who would rise like the sun. Alexandria, known for its great astronomers and their calendrical calculations, was tasked with determining the date of Pascha. At Nicaea, the vernal equinox of the Julian Calendar (based on a 365-day solar rotation) was chosen as the first measurement by which to fix the feast (Pascha falling on the first Sunday after the first full moon after the equinox). Hence, the saint suggests, the lengthening of the day as we move toward the equinox and the ensuing feast is meant to remind us of the true "sun of righteousness," Jesus Christ.

After this beautiful opening, St. Athanasius continues his consideration of time and seasons with an exegetical application of various biblical texts, including Isaiah 49:8, 2 Corinthians 6:2, Exodus 23:14, Psalm 80/81:4; Numbers 10:1–2, 9; and Hebrews 9:10.[4] These Old and New Testament references reveal a transition from the period of the Law and shadow to that of the Savior, presenting us with an understanding of salvation history identical to his fellow Alexandrian and eventual successor as patriarch, St. Cyril.[5]

It is only in paragraph 9 that the saint shifts his emphasis toward ethical exhortation. Building on the verse "sanctify the fast" (Joel 2:15 [translation mine]), he opines regarding those who "dishonour God" and "fast hypocritically."[6] Rather than striving for virtue during Lent, these "defile themselves in the thoughts of their hearts, sometimes committing evils against their brothers and sometimes by daring to defraud." They are the ones who "exalt themselves above their neighbors" and who practice "ostentatious fasting" like the Pharisee

---

4   Ibid., 47–49.
5   Ibid., 49–50.
6   Ibid., 51.

in Luke 18:9–14. The Law offers an antidote to this behavior, commanding humility in the days of fasting (Lev. 23:26–29). Such a fast is "not with the body alone, but also with the soul," for "the soul humbles itself when it is not found among doctrines of wickedness but it feeds on suitable virtues." Saint Athanasius then points to the fasts of Moses on Mount Sinai, Elijah in the desert, and Daniel in Babylon as being worthy of imitation.[7]

The saint briefly returns to his comparison of the Law and its fulfillment in Jesus Christ as he connects the season of Lent with the putting off of old ways in order to be renewed in the Lord. After referencing St. Paul in 1 Corinthians 5:8—who metaphorically correlates the Jewish practice of cleansing the household of leaven before the Passover with the avoidance of sin—St. Athanasius then exhorts his flock to "[strip] off the old human being with his deeds and [clothe] ourselves with the new human being who has been created in God, with humility of mind, a pure conscience, and meditation on the Law night and day."[8] He then wraps up his letter with the official list of dates for the upcoming fast and feast days, which he says foreshadow "the world to come." He concludes with a Trinitarian doxology, and the words of the apostle: "Greet one another with a holy kiss. The churches of Christ greet you" (Rom. 16:16).

Our second encyclical represents a turbulent time in the life of St. Athanasius. After being condemned at the Council of Tyre, he was exiled by the emperor. He briefly returned to his duties after St. Constantine's death in 337 but then was exiled again in 339. "Festal Letter 10", written in 338, reflects the issues of this period and the saint's difficult battle with the ascendant Arians. Rather than beginning with a prolonged and witty theological digression, he immediately addresses the trouble he finds himself in:

---

7   Ibid., 52–53.
8   Ibid., 55.

For although I have been constrained by the afflictions about which you have doubtless heard, and severe trials have been imposed upon me, and the distance has become very great, while the enemies of the truth have been making investigations about us and conspiring to find a writing from us so that by accusing us they might add to the pain of our wounds, nevertheless, because the Lord has strengthened us and comforts us in our afflictions, we are not afraid, not even when we are constrained in the midst of such injuries and plots, to indicate and announce to you our saving Passover, even from the ends of the earth.[9]

He does not ignore his circumstances, nor does he sorrow without hope; rather, he seeks consolation from God. He goes on to couch his suffering in that of Christ, finding benefit in the humility and patience of those who are unjustly abused.

After continuing in this vein until paragraph 20, he begins to address the heresy of the Ariomaniacs (Arians) who "strike the Benefactor with their tongue, blaspheme against the Liberator, and altogether think up one thing after another against the Savior."[10] These have "denied [Christ's] essential divinity":

Because they see that he came forth from a virgin, they doubt that his is truly the Son of God; because they consider that he became human within time, they deny his eternity; because they observe that he suffered for our sake, they do not believe that he is the incorruptible Son of the incorruptible Father; and in general, because he suffered for our sake, they deny the things belonging to his essential eternity.[11]

---

9   Ibid., 107.
10   Ibid., 115.
11   Ibid., 115.

Saint Athanasius does not simply denounce their heresies, but he provides a short theological defense of Nicene Orthodoxy rooted in his interpretation of John 14:11: "I am in the Father, and the Father in me." He comments, "This is the Lord who is seen in the Father and in whom also the Father is seen, who, while he is truly the Son of the Father, at last became human for our sake, so that he might offer himself to the Father in place of us and redeem us through his offering and sacrifice."[12] In other words, the very same Person who is united with the Father—which alludes to the consubstantiality language of the Nicene Creed without directly quoting it—is also the one who became incarnate in order to effect salvation for humankind. It would not be until the 350s that the saint began using the term *homoousios* in his writings, perhaps seeing this as a linchpin around which to rally the Church against the ongoing threat of Arianism.

Although in exile from his episcopal see, St. Athanasius considered it his duty to provide guidance for the dating of the fast and feast days, concluding his encyclical with this standard ending. Although unable to fulfill all his pastoral responsibilities, he strived always to look after the diocese of Egypt to the best of his ability.

The years 346–356 marked a decade of relative peace for the beleaguered man called by his rivals "the black dwarf" (due to his stature and complexion). Returning from exile in triumph, St. Athanasius took to the helm once more, righting the course of the Church. In addition to writing various theological treatises during this period, he continued the practice of penning annual encyclicals prior to the Great Fast. Unfortunately, the surviving letters from this decade are mostly fragmentary, except for "Festal Letter 19," which he composed in 347 shortly after his return. The occasion prompted him to give thanks to God for His providence and for enabling the patriarch to once again freely address his people. He

---

12   Ibid., 116.

then makes use of a trope we have already encountered—the transition from types and shadows to reality—but with an emphasis on contemporary Judaism.[13] We should sharply distinguish his rhetoric here from the antisemitic attacks of late medieval Roman Catholicism or those of the Protestant Reformers such as Martin Luther or Jean Calvin. Whereas for the latter, Jews constituted a minority ethnic group, racially and culturally divided from Europeans, for the early Greek Fathers they were considered heretics in need of conversion. Alexandria in the fourth century contained perhaps the largest Jewish diaspora community in the Roman Empire, which presented the archbishop with a large theological opposition, one he would be inclined to challenge.

After several paragraphs attacking the doctrines of Judaism, St. Athanasius tips his hand, revealing his motive for denouncing Judaism: the rise of a more recent heresy, Arianism. He compares his fellow Nicene proponents to the apostles who remained faithful to Christ, while he typifies the heretics in Judas the betrayer.[14] In the pages of Holy Scripture he sees the same story playing out, with some rejecting the Messiah (i.e., the Jews and Arians) and others suffering for the Lord's sake (i.e., the apostolic Church now represented by St. Athanasius and his supporters). He then concludes the encyclical with his typical calendrical calculations but adds a lengthy list of names designating which bishops have been consecrated to fill various sees throughout the region.

On February 8, 356 at the behest of the pro-Arian emperor Constantius, soldiers attacked the Church of Theonas in Alexandria where St. Athanasius was celebrating a vigil, after which he began another period of exile and intermittent persecution that concluded only in 363. After this, he reigned peacefully until his death in 373.

---

13   Ibid., 159–64.
14   Ibid., 165–66.

The most important encyclical from this period is his "Festal Letter 39" from 367, which Brakke and Gwynn have separated into its own section in their translation. They comment, "It is the only letter for which a substantial Greek excerpt survives, for that excerpt preserves the oldest extant list containing precisely the twenty-seven books of the current New Testament canon."[15] This is because later Church Fathers cited the letter, and it was referenced at the Council of Trullo as an authoritative list. The remaining fragments of the letter have been preserved in Coptic manuscripts.[16] Its introduction and conclusion are missing, so we are left instead with a fascinating exposition on the purpose and meaning of Holy Scripture rather than a standard epistle.

The archbishop starts off with a lengthy description of Jesus Christ as the great teacher who conveys to His disciples the mystery (Eph. 3:3–4) that they in turn have recorded in writing.[17] Although there are heretics who misinterpret these testimonies, he laments (such as the Jews, Arians, and Melitians), he retorts that the Holy Scriptures remain "sufficient to instruct us perfectly." He then mentions that there are certain books in circulation ("the so-called apocrypha") that have been confused with "the books that are canonized" (which is the first recorded use of the verb "canonize" to describe a list of biblical documents).[18] He then commences with a list of approved Old Testament books: the Pentateuch, Joshua, Judges, Ruth, four books of Kingdoms, Esdras, Psalms, Proverbs, Ecclesiastes, Song of Songs, Job, the four Major Prophets, and the twelve Minor Prophets (including Baruch, Lamentations, and "the letter").[19] He then lists all

---

15   Ibid., 231.
16   Most of the *Festal Letters* have been preserved in Coptic and Syriac, with only fragments in Greek.
17   Ibid., 235–38.
18   Ibid., 239.
19   Ibid., 239–40.

twenty-seven books of the modern New Testament canon, including the Apocalypse (Revelation) of St. John.

After this list, St. Athanasius gives a shorter list of books he states "are not canonized, but have been appointed by the Fathers to be read to those who newly join us and want to be instructed in the word of piety."[20] These include the Wisdom of Solomon, Wisdom of Sirach, Esther, Judith, Tobit, the *Didache*, and *The Shepherd of Hermas*. He distinguishes these from the apocrypha, using that term only to describe those books which "are an invention of heretics."[21] He rejects by name the books attributed to Enoch, one to Isaiah, and another to Moses. "For truly," he adds, "the apocryphal books are filled with myths, and it is a vain thing to pay attention to them, because they are vain and polluted voices." In contrast, the Holy Scriptures always point us to those two foundational doctrines of the Church: the Trinity and the Incarnation.[22]

Having outlined the biblical canon, the saint concludes with a few useful recommendations, including that a biblical teacher should "place before those who desire to learn those things that are appropriate to their age."[23] This does not only include the biological age of a person but their spiritual age: "In the case of those who begin to study as catechumens, it is not right to proclaim obscure texts of Scripture as mysteries and be silent about the teaching they need." The Bible is meant to teach them to "hate sin and abandon idolatry" rather than be a puzzle to confound them. They should look to the example of the biblical saints as they themselves strive to put the words of Holy Writ to practice.

With this we end our examination of *The Festal Letters* by St. Athanasius. The practice of publishing circular letters to a single diocese

---

20 Ibid., 240.
21 Ibid., 241.
22 Ibid., 242.
23 Ibid., 244.

or the collective dioceses of a patriarchate remains a common practice in the Orthodox Church today. Like the encyclicals of this great pope and patriarch of Alexandria, they contain practical, ethical, and theological discourse, and remain an important witness to the Orthodox Faith in every age.

St. Basil the Great

THE PRIVATE LETTERS OF THE Church Fathers provide us with a treasure chest of personal thoughts, historical data, and theological engagements. Some were written to theological adversaries in order to challenge their positions, or perhaps (more irenically) to persuade them to consider supporting an Orthodox view. Quite touching are the many private letters of St. Basil the Great, which were later compiled into a single collection. They reflect the emotional and theological range of the saint and have remained an important testimony to Orthodox Christian thought.

This renowned Bishop of Caesarea flourished in the second half of the fourth century; he was born around 330 and reposed in 378. He was raised in Cappadocia (modern Turkey) within a wealthy but generous Christian family that possessed an impressive spiritual pedigree: His maternal grandfather was a martyr under Diocletian, and his paternal grandmother, St. Macrina, was a disciple of St. Gregory Thaumaturgus (the Wonderworker). Both his parents—Basil the Elder and Emilia—are recognized as saints, as are his siblings, Ss. Macrina the Younger, Naucratius, Peter of Sebaste, and Gregory of Nyssa. As a young man, he received an excellent education, completed at Caesarea Mazaca where he met and became a lifelong friend of the future Bishop of Nazianzus, St. Gregory the Theologian. Later, while embarking on a promising career in law and rhetoric, St. Basil met Eustathius of Sebaste, under whose influence he shifted his pursuits toward service in the Church.

Saint Basil gave much of his wealth to the poor and traveled to the great monastic centers in Egypt and the Levant to learn the ascetical life. However, the hermetical life did not appeal to him in the same way as communal living (cenobitic), which inspired him to form a community of brothers on his family's property in Pontus. His friend St. Gregory joined the community for a time and worked with St. Basil while he was there to extract useful passages from Origen's works to comprise a collection they dubbed *The Philokalia* ("Love of the Beautiful").[24] Perhaps St. Basil would have remained a monk had he not been invited to attend the Council of Constantinople in 360, after which he shifted his allegiance away from Eustathius—a semi-Arian who rejected the term *homoousios*—and became a defender of the Nicene Creed. In the ensuing years he was ordained a deacon and then presbyter, and in 370 he was finally consecrated the hierarch of Caesarea, the most important bishopric in Cappadocia. Until his death in 379, he and his friend St. Gregory (who in 372 was also appointed a bishop in the same region) struggled against various forms of Arianism, including the related heresies of Eunomianism and Macedonianism.

In addition to his theological works and epistles, St. Basil's legacy is marked by three remarkable achievements. His *Longer Rules* and *Shorter Rules* for communal life became standard for cenobitic monasticism, influencing the structure of abbeys and convents for centuries to come. The consecration prayer (Anaphora) of the Divine Liturgy attributed to St. Basil is an exquisite example of liturgical poetry, and the Orthodox Church still uses it today. And with the construction of his Basiliad—the world's first public hospital and soup kitchen for the poor—St. Basil inspired the founding of all the social institutions that would later appear from the medieval period until today.

---

24 Not to be confused with the later collection of the same name compiled and edited by St. Nicodemus the Hagiorite.

The standard collection for the letters of St. Basil the Great is the four-volume set translated by Roy Deferrari and first published in 1926 by Harvard University Press under the Loeb Classical Library collection, and it has been reprinted several times since then.[25] The original Greek is provided in parallel on the left page, with corresponding English on the right, which is perfect for the reader who is learning ancient languages to test his or her knowledge. In the Introduction, Deferrari provides a biographical sketch of St. Basil, a bibliography of other important works by the saint, and a breakdown of the origin, dating, and manuscripts of his letters. The footnotes primarily reference biblical citations but occasionally clarify terminology and certain Greek terms. Perhaps the only thing missing from the translation is a commentary or summary of the content of the letters, a difficult task considering how diverse they are. For our purposes we will choose four of these letters (one from each volume) to showcase St Basil's writing style and concerns, which grant us a glimpse into his personality. When done well, private correspondence was meant to convey one's personality to the addressee, not merely data and pragmatics.

Saint Basil wrote "Letter II" (2) around 358 to his dear friend St. Gregory, just after the former had returned to Pontus to pursue a contemplative life. His hope, we know from other correspondence, was to inspire his companion to join him in solitude. To this end, the letter intends to answer St. Gregory's inquiry as to what sort of pattern St. Basil was establishing in his fledgling community, with the intention of inducing him to come and see for himself. The saint begins by acknowledging the letter he received from St. Gregory: "I recognized your letter, just as men recognize the children of their friends by the parent's likeness appearing in them."[26] From the start we see

---

25   *St. Basil: The Letters,* trans. Roy J. Deferrari, vol. 1–4 (Harvard University Press, 1961–62).

26   *St. Basil: The Letters,* vol. 1, 7.

the flowery style he employs for his task. Rather than simply saying, "I received your letter," St. Basil draws an analogy to inform St. Gregory that he has encountered his true character in the words he has penned. Saint Basil wants to assure his friend that the man he has come to know has shown through the text, and this confirms their deep rapport.

With this succinct but powerful opening, St. Basil immediately addresses his friend's concerns:

> For when you say that the nature of our surroundings would not greatly tend to implant in your soul a desire to live with us until you should learn something of our habits and mode of life, it is truly characteristic of your mind and worthy of your soul, which counts all things of this earth as nothing compared with the promised bliss which is in store for us.[27]

Apparently, St. Gregory has not been convinced to join St. Basil solely on the beauty of the Pontian countryside; he wants to know exactly what sort of practices his friend is establishing there. Notice how, in response to this query, St. Basil does not criticize his friend but commends him for being cautious and discerning. Before answering directly, the saint first admits that he is ashamed to speak of his practices because he is only just beginning the monastic struggle. Having only recently "left my life in the city," he writes, he feels like a seasick man who remains ill even after arriving on shore, "for we carry our indwelling disorders about with us, and so are nowhere free from the same sort of disturbances."[28] Yet, he adds, Christ commanded His disciples to deny themselves, take up their cross, and follow Him; therefore he must continue on in his solitude and ascetical struggle.

---

27 Ibid., 7–9.
28 Ibid., 9.

After these preliminary remarks, St. Basil outlines the purpose and goal of the contemplative life, occasionally inserting practical considerations along the way. "We must try to keep the mind in tranquility," he begins, and then he describes the dilemma of life in the world:

> For just as the eye which constantly shifts its gaze, now turning to the right or to the left, now incessantly peering up and down, cannot see distinctly what lies before it, but the sight must be fixed firmly on the object in view if one would make his vision of it clear, so too man's mind when distracted by his countless worldly cares cannot focus itself directly on the truth.[29]

Saint Basil then laments the way in which worldly duties such as marriage and managing a household can prevent one from focusing on the spiritual life. This gloomy assessment is not merely a rhetorical device meant to persuade St. Gregory to join him but a truth revealed in Holy Scripture. Saint Paul writes,

> But I want you to be without care. He who is unmarried cares for the things of the Lord—how he may please the Lord. But he who is married cares about the things of the world—how he may please *his* wife. There is a difference between a wife and a virgin. The unmarried woman cares about the things of the Lord, that she may be holy both in body and in spirit. But she who is married cares about the things of the world—how she may please *her* husband. And this I say for your own profit, not that I may put a leash on you, but for what is proper, and that you may serve the Lord without distraction. (1 Cor. 7:32–35)

---

29   Ibid., 9–11.

Saint Basil's foundational argument is that the contemplative life is rooted in a spiritual "withdrawal from the world" with the purpose of "unlearning the teachings which already possess [the heart], derived from evil habits."[30] Once the mind is set free from its normal cares, it is able to focus on "the contemplation of God."[31] To aid the contemplative in this work, St. Basil recommends "study of the divinely-inspired Scriptures."[32] Both the precepts contained within and the example of righteous men and women can aid the monk in his struggles. The saint then proceeds to illustrate this using Joseph, Job, David, and Moses as exemplars.

Another important theme in St. Basil's letters is prayer, an action that "engenders in the soul a distinct conception of God."[33] Here he defines the indwelling of God as the ability "to hold God ever in memory, his shrine established within us." The theme of remembrance of God is a common trope in patristic literature, particularly in the Neptic Fathers. This does not mean what is commonly understood by memory today, where we conjure up images of a past event or some useful information. Rather, it means to immerse the conscious mind in the presence of God, to become aware of His presence within the moment. This is achieved "whenever earthly cares cease to interrupt the continuity of our memory [i.e., awareness] of him, whenever unforeseen passions cease to disturb our minds, and the lover of God, escaping them all, retires to God, driving out the passions which tempt him to incontinence, and abides in the practices which conduce to virtue."[34]

With the loftier points now made, St. Basil focuses on more practical matters. Conversation with others should not be boorish nor

---

30   Ibid., 11.
31   Ibid., 15.
32   Ibid., 15.
33   Ibid., 17.
34   Ibid., 19.

contentious but should be "without self-display" and attentive to what the other is saying. One's outward appearance should be like that of mourners, without undue concern for hair and clothing. Food should be simple, enough to satisfy hunger without being extravagant. Bread, fruit, and vegetables are best, eaten once daily and joined by prayers of thanksgiving afterward.[35] And regarding sleep, it "should be light and easily broken, such as naturally follows a moderate diet; and it should be interrupted deliberately by meditations on high themes."[36] One such high theme he mentions is "the recollection of past sins," a practice intended to "ward off evil" and turn the soul toward God. With this, St. Basil closes the letter, having offered his dear friend a taste of the monastic life awaiting him in Pontus.

"Letter CXV" (115), subtitled "To the Heretic Simplicia," is a very different sort of work. Deferrari provides some historical context about the situation that prompted the letter, which the scholar finds elaborated in the epistles of St. Basil's dear friend, St. Gregory the Theologian. The trouble began when St. Basil and St. Gregory together decided to consecrate a new bishop for a certain Cappadocian city. This man was the slave of a wealthy woman named Simplicia, who herself was not an adherent to Nicene Orthodoxy. The bishops had not sought Simplicia's permission for the consecration, which enraged her. She therefore began to broadcast threats to both of the Cappadocian saints.[37] According to one story, she even went so far as to publicly humiliate St. Basil. Learning that he had entered a bathhouse to wash, she had her eunuchs and maids steal his towels, which led to an embarrassing scene. However, as the tale goes, these servants later mysteriously died, prompting Simplicia to send money to the saint to make amends—a gesture he adamantly refused.[38]

---

35   Ibid., 23.
36   Ibid., 25.
37   *St Basil: The Letters*, vol. 2, 228.
38   Ibid., 229.

Whether this story actually occurred is hard to say. Regardless, the tone of "Letter CXV," written around 372 or 373, shows a different side to St. Basil. He begins by saying, "I myself now check my tongue, by silence smothering the indignity of the insults offered me."[39] He does not mince words, immediately warning Simplicia how her actions have injured him. Yet he makes it clear that he will not retaliate but leave justice to God: "But I shall await the Judge above, who knows how in the end to avenge all evil." Saint Basil then reminds his interlocutor of what awaits every soul, telling her to "be mindful of the last day, and, if you please, do not try to teach us." He then commences to chastise her actions as well as those of her servants. In particular, he heaps scorn upon her eunuchs, attacking the very nature of their lifestyle: They are "neither feminine nor masculine, woman-mad, envious, of evil wage, quick to anger, effeminate, slaves to the belly. . . . They are chaste without reward—thanks to the knife; and they rave with passion without fruition—thanks to their own lewdness."

These sentiments about Simplicia's eunuchs are perhaps the most severe St. Basil ever expressed. What are we to make of this? Personal correspondence often preserves different facets of an individual's personality, including moments of emotional distress. We see this also in the letters of St. Basil's friend St. Gregory, where we witness his struggles with sadness and his frustration with others. Lest we forget, the Church Fathers were mere mortals, capable of making mistakes or being distressed. This is one of the reasons they are so relatable to us. So we should not judge St. Basil too harshly. By insulting him, Simplicia did not humiliate a simple monk: She mocked the hierarch of Caesarea and therefore maligned his office. It is sometimes the duty of a spiritual leader to humble others for the sake of their salvation. Had Simplicia truly repented, converted from her heresy, and asked

---

39   Ibid., 231.

his forgiveness, we can imagine St. Basil would have gladly received her back into the Church.

Our next work is "Letter CCXXXIV" (234) in volume 3 of Deferrari's translation. Written in January 376, it is one of several epistles to Amphilochius, Bishop of Iconium, this time in answer to the question, "Do you worship what you know or what you do not know?" Saint Basil's response has become a locus classicus of early Christian theology, encapsulating ideas that would be defended by later Fathers down to St. Gregory Palamas in the fourteenth century.

Throughout this letter, St. Basil imagines a heretical group of interlocutors with whom he debates the meaning of God's essence (*ousia*) and activities (*energeia*). If he were to answer the above question saying, "What we know, that do we venerate," they would respond, "What is the essence of that which is worshipped?" And if he were to say the opposite, they would reply, "You worship what you do not know."[40] Thus he must approach the question from a different angle: "But we say that 'knowing' has many meanings." At this point he makes an important distinction: "We say that we know the greatness of God, and His power, and His wisdom, and His goodness, and His providence whereby He cares for us, and the justice of His judgment, not His very essence." But perhaps they should rejoin that this contradicts the simplicity of God. Without rejecting the simplicity of God's unknowable essence, St. Basil doubles down on his doctrine: "But we say that from his activities we know our God, but his essence itself we do not profess to approach. For his activities descend to us, but his essence remains inaccessible."[41]

Saint Basil supplies another riposte from the heretics: "If you are ignorant of the essence of God, you worship what you do not know." To this he eloquently replies:

---

40   *St Basil: The Letters*, vol. 3, 371.
41   Ibid., 373.

But I do know that he exists, but what his essence is I consider beyond understanding. How then am I saved? Through faith. And it is faith enough to know that God is, not what he is, and that he is a rewarder of those who seek him. Knowledge of his divine essence, then, is the perception of his incomprehensibility; and that which is august and comprehended, not as to what his essence is, but that he exists.[42]

To support this claim, he cites John 1:18: "No man has seen God at any time; the Only-begotten, who is in the bosom of the Father, He has declared Him." He asks, "What has the Only-begotten of the Father declared, His essence or His power?" If they say His essence, then where do the Scriptures support this claim? Abraham and the disciples believed in God in response to His activities. Through His working within creation "they knew His divinity" and came to worship Him.[43] Saint Basil then concludes with a powerful statement: "Thus worship follows faith, and faith is strengthened by power. . . . Therefore we believe in Him whom we understand, and we worship Him in whom we believe." In other words, worship of God is not based on the ability to comprehend God's inner life and being; it is a faithful answer to God acting in and through His world. A millennium later, St. Gregory Palamas would necessarily explain this again to his opponent Barlaam.

Our final item for consideration is "Letter CCC" (300), which St. Basil wrote to a grieving father in the early 360s when he was a deacon and teacher. One of his students died unexpectedly, prompting him to write a touching note of consolation. "Since the Lord has set us in the second rank of fathers to Christians," he begins, "having

---

42   Ibid., 375.
43   Ibid., 377.

entrusted to us the molding through religion of the children of those who believe in him, we have considered the calamity which has befallen your blessed son to be also our own."[44] As the boy's pedagogue, he shares the father's "great sorrow of heart." However, he carefully encourages him "to bear these things temperately" and not to mourn beyond measure, reflecting a biblical virtue St. Paul originally espoused: "But I do not want you to be ignorant, brethren, concerning those who have fallen asleep, lest you sorrow as others who have no hope" (1 Thess. 4:13).[45]

In describing the departed lad, St. Basil employs a bit of hyperbole, praising his friendliness, gentleness, calmness, and intelligence, and adding "though one were to say even more than this he would fall short of the truth." That he died young should not be taken as so great a tragedy because he has died before being drawn toward evil. He has avoided the vices and temptations that normally beset young men, such that his untimely death could even be perceived as a blessing. Saint Basil then ends with a bold statement: "Earth has not covered your beloved son but heaven has received him."[46] To this he adds a quote from Job 1:21, which he expands: "'The Lord gave, and the Lord has taken away'; as it has pleased the Lord so it is done: 'blessed be the name of the Lord forever.'"[47] In the fourth century, as today, the Orthodox Church prayed for the souls of departed Christians, leaving the ultimate judgment to God (with the exception of those individuals glorified as saints, who instead pray for us). Saint Basil's opinion of his student is exceptional, moving him to "canonize" the boy (so to speak) in this eulogy.

---

44 *St. Basil: The Letters*, vol. 4, 219.
45 Ibid., 221.
46 Ibid., 223.
47 Ibid., 225.

As we finish our analysis of St. Basil's personal correspondence, we also complete this chapter on patristic letters. Numerous collections of such letters survive, documenting the public and private lives of the saintly men and women the Church honors. By studying these texts, we gain insights into the authors' historical periods, their interests and challenges, and personal characters. Most importantly, we are taught by their wisdom.

CHAPTER 6

Apologetics

O NE OF THE EARLIEST CATEGORIES of patristic literature
took the form of *apologia*, meaning, "to make a defense." The
idea takes its roots in ancient Greek society, with Socrates' *Apology*,
written by Plato, being one of the earliest and most definitive works
in the genre. Socrates understood the purpose of such a work to be a
response to specific accusations. In reaction to his teaching in Athens, he was accused of impiety (not showing proper reverence to
the gods) and corruption of minors (by teaching them to challenge
custom). The method this philosopher set forth in defending himself
from these accusations was the same he employed in many of his dialogues: the art of posing questions. Every query was meant to lead the
questioner more deeply into knowledge in a way that they came to
have a true possession of the truth, rather than simply accepting the
answer on the basis of authority.

This Socratic method of answering allegations formed the basis
for the earliest Christian apologies, which combined pointed questions and answers with vivid analogies in order to persuade readers to
change their opinions. This pattern later evolved into lengthy treatises
where false tenets were simply stated and answered. These became
the blueprints for the famous doctrinal treatises directed against

specific heresies in the conciliar age and beyond (see chapter 7). As we examine this genre of literature, we will discover that apologia can serve three purposes: to affect better relationships with those outside the Church; to persuade outsiders to join the Church; and to protect Christians from heterodox doctrines and practices.

St. Irenaeus of Lyon

BEGINNING IN THE SECOND CENTURY, Christian writers were primarily concerned with dispelling stereotypes that were spreading throughout the Roman Empire. Whispers about secret meetings before dawn and strange rites gave rise to rumors about wild bacchanalia where cannibalism and incest took place (confusing the Eucharist and kiss of peace for grotesque practices). In response to such stories, Roman citizens began to promulgate pogroms against Christians in their respective municipalities. These persecutions were at first localized but gradually grew into larger, state-sanctioned events. Christianity was dubbed illicit, a *superstitio*, and therefore scheduled for eradication. The cruelty of these persecutions reached a crescendo in the third and early fourth century under emperors Decius, Valerian, and Diocletian.

In order to counter false representations of Christianity, the apologists wrote in a manner that would be accessible to those outside the Church. They addressed stereotypes and defended the virtuous actions of Christians hoping to quell the violence brought upon their people. One of the earliest such documents is the anonymous *Epistle to Diognetus*. Although the author does not identify himself in the text, only calling himself "a disciple of the apostles," internal and external evidence suggests that it could be the work of St. Polycarp of Smyrna.[1] According to his own student, St. Irenaeus, St. Polycarp

---

1   See Charles E. Hill, *From the Lost Teaching of Polycarp: Identifying Irenaeus' Apostolic Presbyter and the Author of Ad Diognetum* (Mohr Siebeck, 2006).

(along with St. Papias of Hierapolis) was indeed a direct disciple of one of the apostles: St. John the Theologian. Writing about his youth when he studied under St. Polycarp, St. Irenaeus confirms on two occasions that his mentor studied directly under the apostle.[2] The city of Smyrna was one of several large cities along the western coast of Asia Minor, the same region where St. John settled in his latter years. It also seemed to be the locale of early persecutions, as borne out by the Book of Revelation, which the apostle wrote while exiled to the nearby prison island of Patmos. It was just such oppression that would later inspire this "disciple of the apostles" to pen his apology to a local dignitary in Smyrna named Diognetus.

The author begins by saying that he writes to Diognetus because Diognetus is favorably disposed toward Christians, a good will the author hopes to build upon. But to go further, he tells his recipient: "Cleanse yourself from all the thoughts that are preoccupying your mind, and remove the habit that is deceiving you, and become a new man as through the origin, who is receiving a new word."[3] He then addresses the main reason the Romans despise Christians—because the followers of Jesus refuse to worship idols made of material things: "For this reason you hate Christians, because they do not think that these [idols] are gods. "[4] But why do the Christians not simply identify as Jewish then, he imagines Diognetus responding. The author dismisses this possibility, pointing out that Christians do not make any blood offerings at all, nor do they follow the kosher prescriptions of the Jews.[5] What defines the Church is something radically new,

---

2   *Irenaeus of Lyon*, trans. Robert M. Grant (Routledge, 1997), 179. See also
     Letter to Florinus, an epistolary fragment from St. Irenaeus contained in
     Eusebius, *The History of the Church*, trans. G. A. Williamson (Penguin, 1965),
     168–169.
3   "Epistle to Diognetus," 2.1 (translation mine).
4   Ibid., 2.6.
5   Ibid., 3.2–5.

he explains, and he offers a beautiful description of Christianity in the second century:

> Christians are not distinguished by location nor language nor customs from the rest of mankind. They do not dwell in their own cities, nor speak some strange dialect, nor practice a strange way of life. They do not possess a manmade teaching, nor are advocates of human doctrines (as others are). Inhabiting both Greek and barbarian cities, as each one's lot was cast, they follow the local customs in clothing, cuisine, and other aspects of life. At the same time, they demonstrate an astonishing, and by all accounts, paradoxical lifestyle. They live in their respective countries, but as sojourners; they share in everything as citizens, and endure everything as foreigners. Every foreign land is their homeland, and every homeland is a foreign land. They marry and have children just like everyone else, but they do not kill their offspring. They have a common table, but not a common bed. They find themselves in the flesh, but do not live according to the flesh. They live on earth, but their citizenship is in heaven. They obey the prescribed laws; in their own lives even surpassing the laws. They love all, yet all judge them. They are unknown, and yet they are condemned. They are put to death, and yet are made alive. They are poor, yet make many rich; they are in need of everything, yet they abound in everything. They are dishonored, yet in their dishonor they are glorified; they are slandered, yet they are justified. They are cursed, yet they bless; they are insulted, yet they show honor. When they do good, they are punished as wicked; when they are punished, they rejoice as being rejuvenated. The Jews attack them as strangers and the Greeks persecute them; yet they cannot give a reason for their hatred. Simply put, what the soul is in the body, Christians are in the world.[6]

---

6   Ibid., 5.1–6.1.

For the remainder of his apology, the author dismantles the practices of idolatry, presenting the Christian way as a virtuous and philosophically sound alternative to the ancient Greco-Roman religions of antiquity.

Saint Irenaeus of Lyon is the most important student of St. Polycarp. After being ordained a presbyter, he left Asia Minor to assist the fledgling missions in the Roman province of Gaul (modern France). In 177, St. Irenaeus was sent to Rome by his local bishop, St. Eleutherius of Lyon, carrying a letter warning of the growing heresy of Montanism. Meanwhile, the persecutions of emperor Marcus Aurelius had finally reached Gaul. When St. Irenaeus returned home, he found that his bishop and numerous others had died as martyrs at the hands of Roman soldiers. He was then chosen to succeed St. Eleutherius, serving as a hierarch until his own martyrdom around 202.

The rise of Montanism was not the only theological threat facing the Church in the second century. In the post-apostolic age there began to form numerous sects rivaling Christianity. Some of these were formed by former Christians who left the Church to form their own religion, while others emerged independently of the Church yet were influenced by Christian doctrine, which they syncretized with other religious and philosophical ideas and practices. This gave an impetus to the Fathers to defend the Faith against heresy, to protect the Christian flock, and to persuade those in the sects to join the Church. In Gaul specifically, St. Irenaeus was facing off with the Valentinians, a heretical sect that scholars today identify as Gnostic. The Gnostics were not a singular, organized religion but a cluster of groups throughout the empire that shared certain tendencies: They claimed to profess hidden knowledge about spiritual realities, not known or available to the general populace; they often tended toward extreme practices, either intense asceticism on the one side or moral libertinism on the other; they usually adopted some form of dualism, thereby rejecting the goodness of God's creation; and they rejected the reality of the Incarnation of Jesus Christ and of His saving death and Resurrection.

The influence of the Valentinians must have been great enough to elicit an apology from St. Irenaeus, which appears in five books called *Against Heresies*. These are a treasure trove of early Christian theology and practice, in addition to being a primary source for understanding what the Gnostics believed. Within we have quotes from a majority of the twenty-seven canonical New Testament books, as well as a defense for the use of only the four traditional Gospel accounts. There are also numerous historical references, which provide scholars with data points for understanding the growth and establishment of nascent Christianity. The edition we will reference is the 1997 translation by Robert Grant, which includes an introduction highlighting the life of the saint and his approach to battling the Valentinians. What is missing from this edition is a textual apparatus, which would have aided the reader in unpacking the text. However, the translation is quite readable, and St. Irenaeus himself communicates without using philosophical jargon or long, complex analogies, which makes his writing fairly straightforward. We will focus our attention on the first section of this work (Book One).

Establishing his purpose for writing, St. Irenaeus states in his Preface, "Error is not shown forth such as it is, for fear that when stripped it may be recognized, but is fraudulently adorned with persuasive attire and appears more true than the truth itself, ridiculous to say, thanks to this external appearance to the eyes of the ignorant."[7] Here he defends the necessity of exposing the heresy of the Valentinians: The truth is not unapparent or less obvious than falsehood, but falsehood resorts to deception to fool those who lack training to distinguish it as lies. He has a duty, he adds, to protect his flock from wolves in sheepskins. Book One hence introduces several of

---

7   Grant, *Irenaeus*, 57.

the tenets of the Gnostics, setting the stage for his offensive. He then humorously opines, "I think they are right when they do not want to teach this to everyone in public, but only to those capable of providing substantial payments for such great mysteries."[8]

One of the important arguments St. Irenaeus makes pertains to biblical exegesis. Although the Gnostics were known to produce their own source texts, they also made recourse to the canonical texts, yet they warped their meaning for their own purposes. Saint Irenaeus provides us with perhaps the earliest Christian hermeneutic for unpacking the text. First, he critiques the methodology of his adversaries:

> Such is their doctrine, which the prophets did not proclaim, the Lord did not teach, and the apostles did not transmit. They boast that they have known it more abundantly than anyone else. While citing texts from unwritten sources and venturing to weave the proverbial ropes out of sand, they try to adjust, in agreement with their statements, sometimes parables of the Lord, sometimes prophetic sayings, and sometimes apostolic words, so that their fiction may not seem without witness. They contradict the order and the continuity of the Scriptures and, as best they can, dissolve the members of the truth. They transfer and transform, making one thing out of another, and thus lead many astray by the badly constructed phantom they make out of the Lord's words they adjust.[9]

He then likens their practice to that of someone who takes a mosaic of the king's likeness and rearranges the stones to represent instead a fox or a dog. In similar fashion they wrench biblical verses from their original context and incorporate them into their own theological system. He offers several examples of this, first from the Gospel of

---

8   Ibid., 63.
9   Ibid., 65–66.

John and then from Homer's *Odyssey*. "If anyone takes these verses and restores them to their original setting," he avers, "he will make the system disappear."[10] In other words, replaced in their original context, quotes from the Bible fail to support the strange ideas of the Gnostics. And what's more, every Christian has been given a copy of the original image of the King with which to reconstruct the authentic "mosaic": "the rule of truth, which he received through baptism, unchanged within himself." By remembering the creed confessed at one's conversion, he or she can rightly interpret the Scriptures and likewise detect and reject heretical doctrines.

In the subsequent paragraphs, St. Irenaeus addresses specific teachings of the Gnostic sects, arguing against their ideas using logic, biblical exegesis, and even derision. The latter sometimes manifests itself in what we would today consider an ad hominem attack. However, in late antiquity there was a category of rhetoric called *psogos*, which was considered an acceptable tactic. This method involved the denunciation of opponents by calling their character into question, often by associating the other with offensive behavior. Sometimes this invective took the form of sarcasm or biting insults. Although not effective if used in isolation, when combined with a trenchant case against the other's ideas, it bolstered the efficacy of an argument. For example, St. Irenaeus accuses his adversaries of hanging out at gladiatorial competitions and of being "insatiable slaves of carnal pleasures" who seduce the women joining their ranks.[11] The practice of *psogos* may seem offensive to modern sensibilities where polite discourse and charitable disagreement are standard, but we must be careful not to impose our cultural standards on ancient writers. This tactic would have been expected in any debate.

---

10   Ibid., 70.
11   Ibid., 64.

Reading *Against Heresies* can be simultaneously rewarding and tedious. Juicy morsels of Christian theology are wedged between long sections outlining the bizarre teachings and practices of the Gnostics. For a Christian under the pastoral care of St. Irenaeus, the existence of Valentinians and similar sects was a real and present danger, and they would have benefited greatly by his detailed exposition of such falsehoods. But even the modern reader can learn something from this information. Heresies never die, they are simply repackaged and sold under new names. Just as Arianism is now professed by the Jehovah's Witnesses, so Gnosticism has been incorporated into various pseudo-Christian and New Age systems. As the philosopher George Santayana famously said, "Those who cannot remember the past are condemned to repeat it."

St. John Damascene

WITH THE CESSATION OF ROMAN persecution of Christianity, legally codified in the Edict of Milan of 313, the Holy Fathers shifted their attention away from outside adversaries and toward heresies emerging from within the Church. Doctrinal treatises gradually displaced apologetics and were often structured in similar ways. But in the seventh century, a new rival to Christianity began to emerge. A little-known teacher hailing from the Arabian Peninsula had devised a new religion that incorporated pieces of Christianity and Judaism into it yet remained distinct. His name was Muhammad, and his ideology was dubbed Islam. After his death, traditionally dated to 632, members of Muhammad's entourage vied for power over the newly formed religious group. With the election of Abu Bakr to succeed their leader, the Rashidun Caliphate was formed. His immediate successor, Umar, invaded the Levant in 634, conquering Roman Syria by 638 and establishing Muslim rule over the Christian population. In

661, the Umayyad Caliphate replaced the Rashidun and continued to rule the growing Arab empire until 750.

Saint John was born in Damascus around 676. His father, Sarjun ibn Mansur, was a prominent government official in the Umayyad Caliphate, despite being Christian. (It was common in those days for conquerors to retain the talents of local officials they thought would remain loyal to the new regime.) Saint John came of age in an era of occupation. Although he received a solid education in Greek letters, philosophy, and theology, his exposure to early Islam gave him first-hand experience of the practices and the teachings of the Quran. This equipped him with the knowledge to compare his own faith to that of his overlords and to write the first Christian apologies against Islam.

At some point, St. John rejected life as a court official and joined the famous Mar Saba monastery near Jerusalem, eventually being ordained a hieromonk there. When the great Iconoclastic Controversy erupted in 726, St. John defended the production and veneration of icons, authoring three treatises in defense of the tradition while he was beyond the reach of the Roman Empire. These became primary texts at the Seventh Ecumenical Council held in Nicaea in 787. In addition to theological texts, including his famous *Fount of Knowledge*, St. John also wrote hymns. Two such arrangements attributed to him are the canon for Pascha and the odes chanted at an Orthodox funeral. He reposed peacefully at his monastery in 749.

There are two primary texts ascribed to St. John Damascene dealing with Islam. A majority of scholars consider the first of these, titled "Heresy of the Ishmaelites," to be an authentic text written by the saint himself. It is preserved as a section in his *Fount of Knowledge*, in the chapter that details various heresies. The second text, titled *Disputation Between a Christian and a Saracen*, may in fact be St. John's oral teaching as recorded by one of his students at the monastery. A translation of both texts, with parallel Greek and critical apparatus, is included in Daniel Janosik's *John of Damascus: First Apologist to the Muslims.*[12] The majority of the book covers the life of St. John, his interaction with Islam, and the authenticity of the two texts, with the translations included at the end. Overall, Janosik provides a thorough introduction to both the saint and his response to Islam.

"Heresy of the Ishmaelites" begins with a brief description of the new religion: "There is also a coercive religion of the Ishmaelites which prevails at this time and deceives the people, being the forerunner of the antichrist."[13] Saint John describes the Arabs as both Ishmaelites and Hagarenes, accepting without argument the Muslim claim that they descend from Isaac's son. He also refers to them as "Saracens," a term probably originally referring to tribes living in the Sinai Peninsula, but St. John gives an alternate etymology to it by referring to Hagar's alleged words to the angel, "Sarah has sent me away empty." He traces the history of this people through a period of paganism, when they "worshipped the morning star and Aphrodite," to more recent memory when "a false prophet, called Mamed, sprung up among them."[14] He relays a tradition that Mamed (Muhammad) learned something of the Old and New Testaments from an Arian monk, and then "fabricated his own heresy": "And after ingratiating himself and gaining favor from the people under a false pretense of piety, he spread rumors that a book had been sent down from heaven by God. Thus, heretical pronouncements inscribed in his book and worthy of laughter, were instead handed to them as something to be believed."[15]

The main body of the text outlines Quranic teaching with incredible accuracy and then proffers a Christian rebuttal in return. He underlines that the Quran admits that, although God is one, Jesus is

---

12   Daniel J. Janosick, *John of Damascus: First Apologist to the Muslims* (Pickwick Publications, 2016).
13   Ibid., 260.
14   Ibid., 260–61.
15   Ibid., 261.

still called "the Word of God and his Spirit." The Quran also makes clear that Jesus was conceived miraculously when the Spirit "entered into Mary" and that Jesus did not die upon the Cross but was taken up into heaven. Thus St. John uses their own holy book as his first piece of evidence in his case against them. His next riposte pertains to Muhammad himself: "Who among the Prophets has announced that such a prophet would rise up?"[16] He demands evidence that Muhammad was an authentic prophet of God. By way of contrast, he points out that all the Old Testament saints predicted the advent of Christ—a claim Muslims have no answer to. What's more, they believe that Muhammed received his prophecies while asleep, without any observers around, in violation of the biblical injunction that truth be established in the presence of two to three witnesses.

Saint John then turns his attention to a certain epithet the Muslims call Christians—*etairiastas*, or associators, "because, they say, we introduce in addition to God a partner when we declare that Christ is the Son of God and God."[17] He replies,

> Since you also say that Christ is Word and Spirit of God, why do you accuse us of being Associators? For the Word and Spirit are inseparable from the one in whom they exist by nature. Therefore, if the Word of God is in God, then it is evident that he is God as well. If, however, the Word is outside God, then, according to you, God is without Word and Spirit. Consequently, by avoiding the association of a partner with God, you have mutilated him.[18]

This is the strongest theological defense St. John makes here, pointing out that the Quran contradicts itself in its description of God. In similar fashion, he balks at their claim that Christians worship the

---

16   Ibid., 262.
17   Ibid., 263.
18   Ibid., 263–64.

cross because they show it honor, especially as they themselves venerate the stone housed at the Kaaba.

For the rest of the apology, St. John points to various stories from
the Quran or from the life and sayings of Muhammad (later compiled
as various collections of *Hadith*), picking apart problematic aspects of
these texts. For example, he makes light of the fact that Muhammad's
prophecies personally benefited him, such as the time when God permitted Muhammad to steal the wife of his follower Zayd.[19] He concludes his analysis by listing the practices Muslims have instituted
which directly contradict the evangelical commandments:

> He legislated that they be circumcised, including their wives. He also
> gave a command not to keep the Sabbath and not to be baptized, as
> well as on the one hand, to eat what is forbidden in the Law, and on
> the other hand, to abstain from other things that are permitted. He
> also absolutely prohibited the drinking of wine.[20]

Saint John Damascene's commentary abruptly ends here, having
accomplished a modest refutation of Islam's claims.

In *Disputation Between a Christian and a Saracen*, we find a dialogue between a Christian and a Muslim, similar to early apologetical texts like St. Justin the Philosopher's *Dialogue with Trypho the
Jew*. Structuring a text in this way imagines a real conversation or
debate, hence providing the reader with talking points if they were to
encounter the same questions. Section 1 commences with an important discussion on theodicy. Like Jean Calvin later taught in the six-
teenth century, Islam was concerned with the sovereignty of God.
To believe that humans possess self-determination (as the Church
Fathers taught) was perceived by Muslims as snatching authority

---

19   Ibid., 265.
20   Ibid., 268.

away from God. In the dialogue, the Muslim asks the Christian, "Who do you say is the cause of good as well as evil?"[21] The Christian replies, "We say that God alone is the author of all that is good, but not of evil." Humans are responsible for choosing good or evil, but misuse of their will does not impugn the goodness or authority of God. "If, as you say, good and evil come from God," the Christian states, "then God is unfair; but he is not."[22] The Muslim then rejoins with a question about a conception in the womb that occurs due to fornication or adultery: Does this make God responsible for the sin of the man and woman? The Christian explains that God has given the power of procreation to humans, and therefore He is not responsible for their misuse of this ability.[23]

Section 3 begins a new theme, with an attempt by the Muslim to entrap his Christian opponent. He asks, "In your opinion, is the one who does the will of his God good or evil?"[24] Sensing his ploy, the Christian says, "I know what you are getting at. . . . You want to ask me, 'Did Christ suffer willingly or unwillingly?' So that if I say to you, 'He suffered willingly,' then you will say to me, 'go and bow down before the Jews, for they have done the will of your God.'" The Muslim admits to his subterfuge but still demands an answer. The Christian states, "What you call 'will,' I call 'tolerance' and 'patience.'" The Muslim follows up, asking, "How can you demonstrate that?" Unfortunately, there is a lacuna in the text, so we do not know how the Christian responded. Yet we can imagine that St. John would have provided yet another reasonable refutation. He understood well that, although Orthodox Christian doctrine is not based on rationalism and man-made syllogisms, the revealed truths of the Faith are certainly logically defensible.

---

21   Ibid., 269.
22   Ibid., 270.
23   Ibid., 271.
24   Ibid., 272.

The text picks up again with a discussion similar to that found in *Heresy of the Ishmaelites*, albeit more robust. If the Muslim asks, "Who do you say the Christ is?" the Christian should respond using the term employed in the Quran: "Word of God."[25] Saint John then advises the Christian to turn the same question back to the Muslim and to refuse to move on until he answers. Since Jesus is called Word and Spirit in their own texts, the Christian should add the query, "According to your writings, are the Spirit of God and the Word of God said to be uncreated or created?" This tactic places the Muslim in a bind. If he says "uncreated," he agrees with the Church and can no longer denigrate Christ; but if he says "created," he implies that the Word and Spirit of God came into being at a certain moment. But what if the Muslim asks if the words (in the plural) of revelation are uncreated or created? The Christian should respond "neither," because the Holy Scriptures are "utterances of God" (*rhēmata theou*), not the "one enhypostatic Word of God" (*monon logon tou theou enhypostaton*).[26] Saint John then explains how the Word of God could become man yet remain free of suffering in His divine nature.

The dialogue comes to a close after a few more simple questions, leaving the reader wanting more. But what the Damascene has provided is more than enough to defend the Orthodox Christian Faith from attack. However, some may suggest that an important argument is missing, a tactic frequently utilized in modern evangelical treatments of Islam. Never does St. John conjecture that the Allah, the God of the Muslims, refers to someone other than the God of all, or that he is a pagan deity. In both works, the Christian and Muslim use the Greek term *theos* to refer to the one God, which would have been Allah in Arabic. Historical evidence shows that Arab-speaking Christians used "Allah" to mean God even before Muhammed was born

---

25   Ibid., 273.
26   Ibid., 274.

and used the term to translate *theos* (or the Hebrew *elohim*) from at least the eighth century. Of course, this is not to imply that Muslims then or now have the same conception of God as Christians—they clearly reject the Trinity—but it places Islam in a similar category as rabbinical Judaism, as they pray to a Father they are unable to rightly know because they reject His Son.

Today the discipline of Orthodox Christian apologetics has once again become vogue, particularly in the context of online and social media culture. The writings of the Church Fathers contain the methods and concepts for defending the Faith against a new generation of aggressors. But to those who take up this gauntlet, it is always important to remember the "salvific imperative" that motivated the saints: the desire to protect the reason-endowed sheep of God's flock and to convert adversaries to the apostolic religion.

CHAPTER 7

Doctrinal Treatises

O FTEN WHEN WE ENVISAGE THE Church Fathers, we assume that each of them was a profound theologian, able to easily define doctrine and defend the Faith against heresy. However, this is not always the case. Although every saint had a direct encounter with God and therefore became a recipient of divine wisdom, only some of them were gifted with the ability—and given the opportunity—to engage in the subtle complexities of learning and teaching theology. Those who did have left us numerous doctrinal treatises. With a few exceptions, such as St. John Damascene's *Fount of Knowledge*, these texts originated in the context of controversy, when heresies emerged from within the bosom of the Church. Like apologetical texts, doctrinal treatises addressed falsehoods and offered solutions to theological disputes. They were rarely proactive, formulating new ideas, but were primarily reactive, responding to the challenges of the day.

As this is a broad category of writings, they are not defined by a singular format. Some treatises can be dubbed "discourses," consisting either of lectures delivered publicly or persuasive prose written down. Other treatises are dialogues, capturing either a live debate or a fictitious conversation between two parties. And still others are structured similarly to ascetical literature, containing short passages on various important topics. Whatever the medium, doctrinal treatises remain an important source of theology, with ecclesial councils later approving specific texts or sections from them as authentic representations of Orthodoxy.

For most readers, doctrinal treatises are the most difficult writings to comprehend. They are in-house documents, usually intended for educated clergymen or an astute laity. The rhetorical style of the texts requires greater attention from the reader, as do the abstract concepts and philosophical terminology. For our present examination, we will review two texts produced almost a millennium apart: *The Five Theological Orations of St. Gregory of Nazianzus* and *The Triads* by St. Gregory Palamas. Although they were separated by such a great length of time, we will discover through them the perfect continuity of Holy Tradition within the life of the Church.

St. Gregory the Theologian

Throughout the course of ecclesiastical history, only three men have been honored with the title "theologian": St. John the Evangelist, St. Symeon, and St. Gregory of Nazianzus, whom we now consider. He was born around 329 in Cappadocia to Christian parents, Ss. Gregory the Elder (who would later become Bishop of Nazianzus) and Nonna. The Church also recognizes his siblings as saints: his sister St. Gorgonia and brother St. Caesarius (who died young). Although his mother came from a Christian family, his father converted around the time of the Council of Nicaea in 325, encouraged by his wife's prayers. The younger St. Gregory received an excellent education, which led to his further studies in Athens. There he befriended his fellow Cappadocian, St. Basil the Great—a friendship that continued over the years as they worked together to overcome forms of Arianism.

In 361, St. Gregory was ordained a presbyter to work in his father's diocese. However, he wanted to pursue the contemplative life, and so he left home to join St. Basil at his estate in Pontus. The following year he returned home to assist his father in resolving a controversy in Nazianzus. It was also at this time that the new emperor Julian (dubbed "the Apostate" by Christians) began his campaign to revert the Roman Empire back to paganism. Saint Gregory responded to the emperor's persecution of the Church with his first doctrinal treatise, *Invectives Against Julian*. Eventually, St. Basil convinced his friend to be consecrated Bishop of Sasima in 372.

In 374 his parents reposed, but St. Gregory refused to be chosen as successor to his father's bishopric of Nazianzus. Instead, he gave away his wealth and retreated to a monastery. However, in 379 he accepted an offer to oversee the Pro-Nicene group in Constantinople, at that time independent of the local Church because the temples were under Arian control. Naming the fledgling community Resurrection, they gathered in his home for worship and to hear his series of lectures now known as *The Five Theological Orations*. He remained in Constantinople through 381, when Emperor Theodosius I convened the Synod of Constantinople (Second Ecumenical Council) to resolve the Arian crisis and unify the Church. Saint Gregory was elected president of the council, to the protest of some bishops. In response, he resigned and returned home to Cappadocia, serving a few years as Bishop of Nazianzus before retiring due to poor health. He reposed in 390.

The edition of *The Five Theological Orations* that is often referenced is the translation by Frederick Williams and Lionel Wickham, published under the title *On God and Christ*.[1] Wickham provides a short introduction that provides a biography of St. Gregory and some background information surrounding the Arian controversy and the

---

1   St. Gregory of Nazianzus, *On God and Christ: The Five Theological Orations and Two Letters to Cledonius*, trans. Lionel Wickham and Frederick Williams (SVS Press, 2002).

occasion for the orations. Footnotes after each chapter are mostly biblical references, with a few explanatory notes here and there. Below we will examine the second of these orations ("Oration 28," subtitled "On the Doctrine of God").

Before delving into a difficult discussion about the nature of God, St. Gregory first reminds his hearers what he had told them in his previous lecture. He reviews the stance of his theological rivals the Anomeans, (who were a development out of Arianism). They believe that the Father, Son, and Holy Spirit each consisted of different and incommunicable natures. One of these partisans named Eunomius was even teaching that the human mind could fully comprehend the essence of each divine Person. Saint Gregory questions not only their doctrines but even their ability to undertake the task of theology (as borne out by the irrationality of their premises). Having already taken his adversaries to task in the aforementioned lecture, he then presents a sound exposition on theology beginning with questions about God's essence.

Similar to the allegory sketched in the famous *Life of Moses* by his friend St. Gregory of Nyssa, the Nazianzen compares his theological task with that of Moses entering into the cloud on Mount Sinai. There, "detached from matter and material things" he hopes to hide in the cleft of the rock and catch a glimpse of the "averted figure of God."[2] But in contemplating God, he says he is unable to spy the "nature prime, inviolate, self-apprehended," that which is "hidden by the cherubim," but rather only that which "reaches us at its furthest remove from God." This is the "majesty inherent in the created things he has brought forth and governs" rather than the essence of God. Despite what Eunomius was teaching, it is impossible to apprehend God according to His own manner of existence:

---

2   Ibid., 39.

To tell of God is not possible, so my argument runs, but to know him is even less possible. For language may show the known if not adequately, at least faintly, to a person not totally deaf and dull of mind. But mentally to grasp so great a matter is utterly beyond real possibility even so far as the very elevated and devout are concerned, never mind the slack and sinking souls.[3]

If this is the case, how can a human being know anything about God? We observe God acting in and through His creation: "That God, the creative and sustaining cause of all, exists, sight and instinctive law informs us—sight, which lights upon things seen nobly fixed in their courses, borne along in, so to say, motionless movement; instinctive law, which infers their author through the things seen in their orderliness."[4] The cosmos itself is witness to the God who made and sustains it.

But what about St. Gregory's opponents? What can they determine about God through deductive reasoning or a "closely-scrutinized argument"?[5] Saint Gregory says they attempt to "boast over infinity" and therefore limit the unlimited, rendering God corporeal. In other words, the Anomeans reduce the nature of God to something like the nature of created beings. God is perceived as yet another thing within a universe of things, a "fifth element" but an element nonetheless.[6] The only rational answer is that God is incorporeal (bodiless). Yet even this description cannot contain or limit God in any way, nor can terms such as "ingenerate, unoriginate, immutable, and immortal," which only speak apophatically about what God is not.[7]

---

3   Ibid., 39–40.
4   Ibid., 40–41.
5   Ibid., 41.
6   Ibid., 42.
7   Ibid., 43.

After this, St. Gregory gives a lengthy description of the origin of pagan idolatry, which coincidentally mirrors the historical sequence posited by many modern anthropologists: a gradual evolution from awe at the forces of nature and the veneration of departed family members or local heroes, to the worship of deities representing the cosmos or human values. But now, the Theologian tells us, it is time to reject these fabrications; "God-derived reason" has "led us up from things of sight to God."[8] Returning to his earlier thread he comments, "No one has yet discovered or ever shall discover what God is in his nature and essence." Yet here he adds something mysterious:

> As for a discovery some time in the future, let those who have a mind to it research and speculate. The discovery will take place, so my reason tells me, when this God-like, divine thing, I mean our mind and reason, mingles with its kin, when the copy returns to the pattern it now longs after. This seems to me to be the meaning of the great dictum that we shall, in time to come, "know ever as we are known" (1 Cor. 13:12). But for the present what reaches us is a scant emanation, as it were a small beam from a great light—which means that anyone who knew God or whose knowledge of him has been attested in the Bible, had a manifestly more brilliant knowledge than others not equally illuminated.[9]

With this he recounts several Old Testament theophanies where the patriarchs and prophets encountered "God but not God."[10]

Based on the above passage, some have conjectured that St. Gregory believed that knowledge of God qua God (i.e., according to His essence or divine nature) is only impossible in the present age but becomes a possibility in the age to come. They then cite him

8   Ibid., 49.
9   Ibid., 49–50.
10   Ibid., 50.

in support of a Roman Catholic doctrine called in Latin *visio beat-ifica* (beatific vision) or contemplation of God's hidden essence (as Thomas Aquinas defined it). However, this cannot be the case. First, the beatific vision is said to be obtainable by the saints in the present age, whereas St. Gregory is speaking hypothetically and cautiously about something in the age to come. Second, although St. Gregory does indeed refer to mental apprehension of God, he makes clear that this would only be possible for that mind conformed to the pattern it was made according to, which is Christ. The human nous, when it "mingles with its kin," being united to Christ by grace, is able to know God in ways impossible before the bodily resurrection and final judgment. And third, after providing a long and poetic digression about what humans can perceive in the natural world, St. Gregory concludes with a description of what the angels see: "They hymn God's majesty in everlasting contemplation of everlasting glory." He does not say they behold the essence but rather the glory. This jibes with numerous statements we find in the Church Fathers, culminating in the dogma of the distinction of the essence and activities in the Palamite, or Fifth Council of Nicaea, in the fourteenth century.

This sampling from "Oration 28" is just a taste of the profound theological ideas contained in this series of lectures. Saint Gregory the Theologian, truly worthy of his moniker, is one of the most important Church Fathers to study if one is trying to make sense of complicated dogmas such as the Incarnation and the Trinity. His words push the reader beyond any presuppositions and challenge any facile conceptions. Be advised: read slowly, carefully, and with much prayer.

St. Gregory Palamas

BORN TO AN ARISTOCRATIC FAMILY in 1296, St. Gregory was raised in the courts of Emperor Andronikos II Palaiologos. The emperor personally saw to the boy's education after his father's death, which was the most superb education possible in the Late Byzantine era. But in spite of his patron's hope that he assume a position at court, St. Gregory left for the monastic republic of Mount Athos at the age of twenty-one. There he would be tonsured a monk at the famous Vatopedi Monastery, remaining there several years before transferring to the Great Lavra on the southern tip of the peninsula. Eventually he joined an associated skete in order to immerse himself in hesychasm—a life of ceaseless prayer and the acquisition of inner stillness. He remained there until 1326, when he and his fellow monks left for Thessalonica due to a Turkish invasion.

In 1330, a Calabrian Greek named Barlaam arrived in Constantinople and established himself as a teacher of philosophy and theology. One of his published treatises on the Trinity adopted a radically apophatic view, asserting not only that God's essence cannot be known (a traditional idea) but that humans in fact cannot know God at all. Saint Gregory read and responded to Barlaam in a work called *Apodictic Treatises*, which resulted in a heated intellectual battle between the two. For his part, Barlaam not only defended his peculiar thesis but also attacked the hesychastic life of the Athonite monks, whom he called "navel-gazers" (a pejorative still used today to describe spiritual seekers). This counteroffensive inspired St. Gregory to pen *The Triads in Defense of Those Who Practice Sacred Quietude*, a monumental work that not only defends hesychasm but also provides a solid theological framework concerning the knowledge of God according to His activities rather than His essence (based upon a florilegia of earlier Church Fathers).

Tensions between Barlaam and St. Gregory continued as they volleyed missives back and forth, which lead to a series of synodal meetings from 1341 to 1351 to resolve the matter. The decision of these regional councils—which endorsed the theological position of St. Gregory—later received ecumenical status in the Orthodox Church.

Saint Gregory Palamas reposed in 1359 and was canonized only nine years later. A condemnation of Barlaam's teaching and a defense of the "essence–energies distinction" was subsequently added to the Synodikon of Orthodoxy (read annually on the Sunday of Orthodoxy), and St. Gregory was eventually assigned an additional commemoration on the second Sunday of Lent (displacing St. Polycarp of Smyrna who had previously been honored that day).

Incomplete Greek editions and English translations of *The Triads* were published during the twentieth century. The first complete critical edition of all nine discourses in the original Greek was published by Panayiotis Chrestou in 1962. A full translation into English by Fr. Peter Chamberas was published in 2021.[11] Father Chamberas added a helpful introduction and included footnotes throughout the text for biblical and patristic references. We will utilize this translation in our brief analysis of the second discourse in the third section.

Saint Gregory wrote the "First Triad" separately from the second and third sections, which he added later as his debate with Barlaam intensified. It is structured around three questions: Should the monk pursue secular knowledge? How should the monk enclose his mind within the body? And what is the experience of the uncreated light the hesychasts speak of? To each of these queries, St. Gregory gives a lengthy reply. The "Second Triad" further elaborates on these themes, with the subsections titled "The Wisdom of God and the Wisdom of the World," "The Sacred Quietude and Ceaseless Prayer," and "The Divine and Uncreated Light." Saint Gregory elegantly defends the spiritual experience of the hesychastic monks and their participation in the glory of God.

Finally, in the "Third Triad," he delves more deeply into the dogmatic distinction for which he is famous. The first discourse

---

11   St. Gregory Palamas, *The Triads: In Defense of Those Who Practice Sacred Quietude*, trans. Peter A. Chamberas (Newfound Publishing, 2021).

in this section puts a question to Barlaam: If you agree that what is communicated to the saints is called "divinity," how can the grace of God be created? Citing numerous sources—including St. Macarius the Great, St. Maximus the Confessor, St. Dionysius the Areopagite, St. Basil the Great, St. Symeon Metaphrastes, St. Gregory the Theologian, St. John Chrysostom, St. Gregory of Nyssa, St. John Damascene, St. Andrew of Crete, and St. Symeon the New Theologian, as well as several traditional Byzantine liturgical texts—he makes an airtight case proving that theosis is real participation in the uncreated life of God.

We will focus our attention on the second discourse of the "Third Triad," subtitled "The Essence and Energies of God." Here St. Gregory explains why participation in uncreated grace cannot be union with the very essence of God. He again emphasizes, as he has in the previous discourses, that the saints indubitably see the glory of God when their nous is illuminated. He cites the passage from St. Gregory the Theologian's "Oration 28," which we have already examined, pointing out that the angels indeed see this very same uncreated glory.[12] But Barlaam apparently taught that "one thing alone is unoriginate and eternal, the essence of God; everything else is of a created nature." Saint Gregory ripostes that, if this were true, then

> nothing that is about this essence is eternal and there was a time when all such things did not exist, since the only unoriginate, according to you, is the essence of God. Consequently, there would thus be a time when God the Father did not exist, for this God the Father is not the essence but the one who is around and about, beside and related to the essence. If, however, the Father exists eternally and his unbegotten mode of existence is without beginning, and if you say only the essence of God is without beginning, then this unbegotten mode

---

12 Ibid., 308.

becomes precisely the essence of God—and this notion then is the very chief heretical doctrine of Eunomius![13]

Lurking behind Barlaam's ideas seems to be a Scholastic conception of absolute divine simplicity, a view that sees God as synonymous with His essence. In the previous century, Roman Catholic theologian Thomas Aquinas had defined God as *actus purus* ("pure actuality"); whether Barlaam was directly influenced by these ideas when he lived in Italy is hard to say. Regardless, St. Gregory points out why this is problematic: If we cannot make any distinction in God, and only His essence is eternal and unoriginated, then we cannot even speak of the three Persons (*hypostases*) as uncreated. Behind St. Gregory's reply is also a dictum of ontology in the Greek Fathers, namely that something like a raw essence cannot exist; essence must be hypostasized and exist as a specific instantiation of being, or else it does not exist at all.

If Barlaam admits at least that God's essence is without beginning, St. Gregory continues, then he should also admit that God's essential faculties are also without beginning, or else he accuses God of changing.[14] But if, as St. Gregory posits, God already possesses these powers, then "they are necessarily and always inherent to the one divine essence."[15] He then cites several Church Fathers who stated explicitly that God's activities are without beginning, including His life, virtue, holiness, goodness, and immortality.[16] God is fully present in each of His activities, and "we give names to God on the basis of each one of these, while at the same time affirming that essentially he transcends all of these." But perhaps there are energies of God that enter into and out of existence, such as His creative power? "There are some

---

13   Ibid., 308–9.
14   Ibid., 309.
15   Ibid., 310.
16   Ibid., 311.

energies of God which have a beginning and an end, as all the saints affirm," including His power to create the cosmos out of nothing.[17] Even so, such powers did not truly have a beginning and ending; they are potential energies that become "outward activity" when God acts at certain points.

The distinction between the "infinitely infinite" essence and the natural and unoriginate energies explains why "God is everywhere, contains everything, and is not contained by anything."[18] What is really at stake, for St. Gregory, is whether human beings can actually participate in the eternal and uncreated life of God, not a created intermediary of some sort. This is the only way to make sense of biblical passages describing the indwelling of the Spirit.[19] He confidently proclaims, "I do not believe that anyone will disagree that, on one hand, we have the transcendent super-essential essence that is completely incommunicable, and, on the other hand, we have the illuminations that are energies of that essence, that is, divine energies destined to be received and participated in by the faithful." This makes union with God possible, "physical with physical things, noetic with noetic things."

Even so, the uncreated light of God is itself beyond physical and noetic perception, entirely transcendent but "made present only by divine grace in the rational natures that have been purified." In other words, no creature possesses an innate ability to apprehend God, either with the physical senses or the mind; only God can deign to reveal Himself to His servants, when and as He sees fit. In the paragraphs that follow, St. Gregory answers possible objections and provides analogies and citations to bolster his argument. He makes clear that true knowledge does not come from mental exercises (such as comparing apophatic and cataphatic descriptions) but from actual

---

17   Ibid., 312.
18   Ibid., 313, quoting St. Cyril as referenced in St. Maximus's *Letter to Marinus*.
19   Ibid., 317.

interaction with God.[20] Here he sets the stage for the third discourse in this section, which will concentrate on the encounter with God through His uncreated energies.

Far from pandering innovation, St. Gregory Palamas was a great synthesist of the Church Fathers. He was able to properly encapsulate the Orthodox Church's teaching not because he was intelligent and educated—although he was both—but because he embodied the hesychastic life himself, spending years in ascetical struggle on the Holy Mountain. His defense of the Faith was not an abstraction, like Barlaam's theories, but an expression of his own encounter with the uncreated God who had revealed Himself to a lowly monk. Saint Gregory remains the most important theologian of the twilight years of the Eastern Roman Empire, a perfect embodiment of the patristic mindset.

---

20   Ibid., 319.

CHAPTER 8

Catechism

RELIGIOUS INSTRUCTION HAS ALWAYS BEEN a part of Orthodox Christian life. In Acts, we are given a snapshot of the early Church, "And they continued steadfastly in the apostles' doctrine and communion, in the breaking of bread, and in the prayers," (2:42 [my translation]) where education is ranked alongside participation in the Sacraments as a sine qua non of Christian life. For those who were not yet baptized, or for youth being raised in the Church, teachers focused on the primary doctrines of the Faith as summarized in various creeds (later merged into the singular Nicene Creed) and basic practices of Christian living. This process became known as *catechism*, from a Greek compound word combining *kata* and *ēchos*, meaning "according to the voice," i.e., to teach orally. The earliest surviving catechetical text is a segment in a first century text called the *Didache*, or "Teaching of the Apostles," and emphasizes those behaviors which should be normative for a Christian. Later catechetical texts added explanations of important dogmas or summaries of biblical truths. They may have also included a section meant to be taught after Baptism called mystagogy, which provided a deeper exploration of the Sacraments the newly illumined believer had just been initiated into.

Over the centuries, some catechetical documents also became important witnesses of Orthodox theology, such as the *Longer Catechism* by St. Philaret of Moscow. Others were relegated to bookshelves and rarely if ever utilized. This is because the practice of catechism is ever evolving. The teacher must adapt to the needs of his or her students and use models and metaphors that are recognizable to the catechumens. What is helpful for those converting to Christianity from another religion may not aid those leaving a heterodox Christian confession. What can be understood by an adult may not be by a child. And what was taken for granted by peoples living in earlier eras may not be by a contemporary generation. Catechetical texts have therefore been designed with the needs of the student in mind. To gain an appreciation for this genre of patristic literature we will examine two classic works: *The Catechesis* by St. Cyril of Jerusalem and the *Catechetical Discourse* by St. Gregory of Nyssa.

St. Cyril of Jerusalem

THE CHURCH OF JERUSALEM IN the fourth century was a small yet influential bishopric. After the famous Levantine pilgrimage of St. Elena (mother of St. Constantine the Great) from 326–328, and her discovery of the True Cross of Jesus Christ, the old city became a destination for spiritual seekers, as evidenced in the travelogue of the Spanish nun Egeria who recorded her own pilgrimage to Jerusalem in the 380s. The hierarch of Jerusalem at that time was St. Cyril, whose reign began sometime around 350. Not much more is known about his early life. Although he supported the Council of Nicaea, he was for decades unconvinced of the utility of the term "homoousios" (finally publicly endorsing it at the Second Ecumenical Council about five years before his death). During his tenure as bishop, he was exiled at least three times, which reminds us of the attacks St. Athanasius endured in the same century.

The surviving works we have from St. Cyril, in addition to his *Cat-echesis*, are his *Mystagogy, Sermon on the Paralytic, Letter to Constan-tius*, and various fragments. English versions of these texts appear in *The Works of Saint Cyril of Jerusalem* in two volumes, translated by Leo McCauley.[1] McCauley provides a thorough introduction, including a short life of the saint and details concerning his milieu, an exposition on his understanding of knowledge of God vis-à-vis biblical exege-sis, and a discussion concerning creeds in the early Church. Foot-notes for the primary text are mostly references, with the occasional explanatory note. In general, McCauley allows the text to speak for itself. We will briefly outline the themes in the "Proto-Catechesis" (an introductory sermon) and eighteen catechetical lectures of St. Cyril, citing some salient passages along the way.

The first talk St. Cyril gives, the "Proto-Catechesis," is meant to ready the catechumens for what lies ahead. They are entering into the Great Fast in preparation for Pascha and now have been registered as candidates for Baptism at the culminating feast. In addition to attending the bishop's lectures, they must undertake the strict asceti-cal practices of Lent and undergo regular exorcisms. They will mem-orize the baptismal creed and internalize the doctrines of the Faith. The bishop warns them that they must not take any of this lightly, lest they risk the condemnation of Simon Magus (Acts 8:13) who, due to insincerity, "was dipped in the font, but he was not enlightened."[2] He exhorts them to attend the lectures diligently and maintain both external and internal silence so that they may imbibe the lessons.[3] "Great is the prize set before you in baptism," he says, "ransom of captives, remission of sins, death of sin, a new spiritual birth, a shin-ing garment, a holy seal inviolable, a heaven-bound chariot, delights

---

1   *The Works of St. Cyril of Jerusalem*, trans. Leo McCauley, 2 vols. (Catholic University Press, 1968 and 1970).
2   McCauley, vol. 1, 71.
3   Ibid., 78–80.

of Paradise, a passport to the kingdom, the grace of the adoption as sons."⁴ Yet a dragon lurks along the path, ready to pounce on them, he warns. They must be careful if they intend to finish the course. Ignore the temptations of the world and all its ruses, he advises them.⁵ He then concludes with a prayer and doxology: "May [God] fill you with the heavenly treasures of the New Covenant, and sign you with that seal of the Holy Spirit, which no man shall break forever, in Christ Jesus our Lord, to whom be glory forever and ever. Amen."⁶

While "Lecture 1" reprises St. Cyril's introductory comments, "Lecture 2" addresses the particulars of a pious Christian life. He begins with a quote from Ezekiel 18:20–21 and then defines sin as "an evil freely chosen, the product of the will."⁷ Because it is voluntary, "it corrodes the fiber of the soul and makes it liable to eternal fire." But where did this inclination come from? The saint offers a summary of salvation history, pointing out that the devil sinned first and then drew Adam into his nets by tempting him to do the same.⁸ "To those who hearken to [the devil], he suggests evil desires, whence arise adultery, fornication, and every kind of evil. By his agency our forefather Adam was cast out and exchanged a Paradise that, untilled, produced fruits for a soil bringing forth thorns."⁹ Following a common tradition in the Orthodox Church, St. Cyril describes sin as illness, but he reminds us that humans' "wounds are not beyond the healing of the great Physician."¹⁰ Through repentance, Christ is able to forgive the sinner. Saint Cyril then chronicles the many instances in the Bible where God showed mercy to his servants, including Adam, Aaron, Rahab, David, Solomon, Jeroboam, Isaiah, and the Three

---

4   Ibid., 82.
5   Ibid., 83.
6   Ibid., 84.
7   Ibid., 96.
8   Ibid., 98–99.
9   Ibid., 99.
10   Ibid., 99.

Holy Youths in Babylon.[11] Saint Cyril's teaching is firmly rooted in scriptural exegesis, not simply abstract doctrines.

"Lecture 3" offers a brief exposition on the meaning of Baptism, connecting the Sacrament to the primordial waters of creation and the hovering of the Spirit in Genesis 1. After alluding to other biblical images of water, he clarifies why the Baptism of the Church is unique: "Jesus sanctified baptism when He himself was baptized."[12] He adds, "Not that He was baptized to receive the remission of sins—for He was without sin—but being sinless, He was nevertheless baptized that He might impart grace and dignity to those who receive the sacrament."

With his next talk, "Lecture 4," St. Cyril summarizes the Christian Faith as ten principles. These will provide the framework for his subsequent sermons, each dealing with aspects of Orthodox teachings unpacked in more detail and with reference to Scripture and the Nicene Creed. "True religion," he insists, "consists of these two elements: pious doctrines and virtuous actions."[13] In modern terms we might call this theory and praxis—two halves of a whole, equal in importance. Of the necessary doctrines a catechumen must know, St. Cyril lists: (1) "That God is one alone, unbegotten by another"; (2) that Jesus Christ is "the one and only Son of God . . . begotten God of God"; (3) "that this Only-begotten Son of God came down from heaven to earth for our sins, taking on this passible human nature of ours, being born of the Holy Virgin and the Holy Spirit"; (4) that Christ "was truly crucified for our sins"; (5) that Christ "was truly laid as man in a rock tomb"; (6) that "He who descended to the regions beneath the earth ascended again, and the Jesus who was buried rose again truly on the third day"; (7) that Christ "ascended again into heaven"; (8) that Christ will come to "judge the living and the

---

11   Ibid., 100–107.
12   Ibid., 115.
13   Ibid., 120–21.

dead"; (9) that the "Holy Spirit is one and indivisible"; and (10) that a human being is bipartite, "composed of soul and body."[14]

The saint then elaborates further on the soul (*psychē*), the animating life force of a person—which he asserts is immortal not by nature but because God "makes it to be immortal." When a person first comes into being, his or her soul "has committed no sin" and therefore is only culpable for later transgressions. "The soul possesses freedom; and though the devil can make suggestions, he has not the power to compel against the will."[15] Saint Cyril then speaks of the body, dismissing dualists who would assert "that this body of ours is a stranger to God."[16] In fact, the body is not the cause of sin but rather the life that animates it is responsible. "The body is the soul's instrument, its cloak and garment. If then it is given up to fornication by the soul, it becomes unclean; but if it dwells with a holy soul, it becomes a temple of the Holy Spirit."[17] To support this, he offers an excursus on the practice of chastity, which is fortified by moderation in food and drink (as well as fasting) and preference for plain apparel.[18] Care must be taken in daily life because this same body will be raised on the last day.[19]

Saint Cyril wraps us his lecture with a few comments about the Bible. First, he affirms that the teaching he has received is not novel but "that of the divinely-inspired Scriptures, both of the Old and the New Testament."[20] To anyone who would reject the Old Testament, he says, "Quote that saving word against him: Jesus came not to destroy the Law, but to fulfill it." Regarding the text, he cites the legendary origin of the Septuagint from the *Letter of Aristeas* as evidence of its divine origin. "Of these," he adds, "read the twenty-two books,

---

14   Ibid., 119–28.
15   Ibid., 129.
16   Ibid., 130.
17   Ibid., 131.
18   Ibid., 131–33.
19   Ibid., 133.
20   Ibid., 135.

and have nothing to do with the apocryphal writings. Study earnestly only those books which we read openly in the Church."[21] To these he appends the New Testament texts. His final list is almost identical to that of St. Athanasius in his festal letter of 367, except that he includes Esther and omits St. John's Revelation. As for any work not read publicly in worship, these should be put in "second rank" and "not read by yourself." In other words, certain books are not forbidden, per se, but catechumens should not study them until a teacher believes they are ready to be guided through them.

The remainder of the *Catechetical Lectures* of St. Cyril expand the doctrinal themes already set forth. By the end of the Great Fast, the catechumens would have become "baptizands": candidates for the Sacrament of Christian initiation. After Pascha they would have been enjoined to attend the services daily during Bright Week, donning their pristine white tunic as a symbol of their purity and the effulgence of the Holy Spirit. Between services, St. Cyril would lecture on the deeper meaning of the Sacraments, a series called the *Mystagogy*. This information was kept hidden from the public, according to the evangelical injunction, "Do not give what is holy to the dogs; nor cast your pearls before swine, lest they trample them under their feet, and turn and tear you in pieces" (Matt. 7:6). But after the high holy days came to a close, the newly illumined Christians would have returned to their worldly affairs. Now the real work would begin: denying themselves, picking up their cross each day, and following after Christ.

St. Gregory of Nyssa

WE HAVE ALREADY MET TWO of the three Cappadocian Fathers: St. Gregory the Theologian and St. Basil the Great. Now we meet the

---

21   Ibid., 136.

younger brother of the latter and completion of the set, St. Gregory of Nyssa. He received a similar education to his sibling but pursued a secular career as a teacher of rhetoric, only entering into ecclesiastical affairs in 371. This was at the insistence of St. Basil, who arranged for him to be consecrated as hierarch for the city of Nyssa in Cappadocia. As the times were turbulent, St. Gregory was persecuted on more than one occasion, being deposed and eventually restored to his episcopacy. He reposed peacefully in 394. Although his clerical career was relatively unremarkable in comparison to his Cappadocian peers, his theological writings reflect the mind of a profound thinker, as we will assay.

In *Catechetical Discourse: A Handbook for Catechists*, Fr. Ignatius Green provides us with a full translation of St. Gregory's catechesis as well as a hefty introduction that delves into the saint's thought.[22] Of note is the editor's examination of the Nyssen's views concerning *apokatastasis* ("restoration"), wherein he defends St. Gregory against those who would ascribe an Origenian form of universalism to him. It is a helpful discussion and a good example of an Orthodox approach to patristics. In the body of the text, the English translation is accompanied by the original Greek critical edition in parallel; and the footnotes contain not only citations but also numerous explanatory comments. There is also a handy Greek-English glossary in the back.

Unlike St. Cyril in his *Catechetical Lectures*, St. Gregory is not here offering instruction directly to catechumens. As the title of the volume implies, he is providing a manual for catechists, mentoring them in both technique and content. The first section envisions the catechist as apologist, answering the objections of future converts coming to Christianity from diverse backgrounds. He proffers advice on

---

22 *Saint Gregory of Nyssa: Catechetical Discourse, A Handbook for Catechists*, trans. Ignatius Green (SVS Press, 2019).

speaking with pagan Greeks about the unity of God and the three Persons, and to Jews about the Word and the Spirit as found in their Scriptures.[23] Then the second, third, and fourth sections expound various theological themes and address possible objections from students. We will examine a few interesting passages from the text to provide a sample of its brilliance.

Theodicy remains one of the most debated subjects in modern religion and seems to have been just as important in late antiquity. Presaging the response of a student, St. Gregory writes, "'Whence is it, then,' you ask, 'that he who was honored with the best of all things exchanged good things for inferior ones?'" That is to say, why did Adam reject the gifts of Paradise and choose evil instead? Implied in the question is an accusation against God. But the Scriptures, he responds, make clear that God is not responsible for evil:

> Evil is somehow implanted within [a person], being composed by decision then, where there is any withdrawal of the soul from the good. For just as sight is an activity of nature, and blindness is a privation of a natural activity, so too virtue is opposed to vice. For the genesis of vice is to be understood in no other way than as an absence of virtue. For just as when the light is taken away darkness follows, but when [light] is present [darkness] does not exist, so as long as good is present in a nature vice is in itself something nonexistent, but the withdrawal of what is superior is the genesis of the opposite.[24]

Evil is not something that exists in and of itself. It is the absence of goodness, the twisting or distortion of what God made to be good. (The analogies St. Gregory provides—blindness and darkness— become common tropes in Orthodox theology to describe what

---

23   Ibid., 62–71.
24   Ibid., 76.

evil is, or what it is not). But if God is good, then, and He created the angels and human beings to reflect this goodness, why did we fall? The rupture between God and sentient beings began with a moment of "turning away from goodness," a misuse of the will that results in wickedness.[25] The devil did this when he began to envy man; and once "torn from an innate affinity with the good and weighed down toward vice on his own initiative," he turned his wrath upon Adam, "persuading him to become his own murderer and executioner."[26]

Saint Gregory then puts forward another objection: If God is omniscient, did He not foresee the fall of Adam and Eve, and thus is He not responsible for allowing it? Saint Gregory releases God from culpability, explaining, "He did not put human nature under the yoke of some necessary compulsion to his own good pleasure, dragging it to the good as if it were an inanimate, unwilling vessel."[27] God creates us free and does not force us to direct our will toward what is good: "But if someone, while the light shining freely on a clear day, should willingly close his eyes, the sun is outside the cause of not seeing."[28] The good news is that people can direct this same freedom back toward God. Although the physical body is condemned to death, humans may be "reformed by the resurrection to the form [he had] from the beginning, if indeed he preserves what is according to the image in the present life."[29]

Later in the *Catechetical Discourse*, St. Gregory submits another objection for consideration: Why was the entire dispensation of history and work of Christ necessary? Could not God simply have saved humankind by fiat? Before answering, the Nyssen outlines how God

---

25   Ibid., 78.
26   Ibid., 79–80.
27   Ibid., 82.
28   Ibid., 82–83.
29   Ibid., 84.

could enter into human existence without succumbing to vice in any way. Then he finally makes his main point:

> For when our nature, through its own proper order, was changed in [Christ] also, in the division of soul and body, he again joined together what was divided as if with some sort of glue—I mean by divine power—fitting together what was torn apart in an unbreakable union. And this is the resurrection: the return, after dissolution, of things that had been conjoined into an indissoluble union, so they grow together with each other, so that humanity's first grace might be recalled and that we might return again to eternal life, the vice mixed in [our] nature having flowed out through dissolution, as happens in the case of a liquid when the vessel holding it is broken—it is dispersed and disappears, since there is nothing to contain it.[30]

The solution God has provided is to heal our nature from the inside out. By joining His divine, eternal life to human flesh, Jesus Christ has overcome the power of death; hence mortality will be abandoned in the grave when the universal resurrection dawns. If this explanation is not sufficient for the inquirer, St. Gregory quips, "Say something like this to reasonable people: that those who are sick do not legislate the manner of care for physicians."[31]

There are many other wonderful exchanges in the *Catechetical Discourse*, including St. Gregory's characterization of the death and Resurrection of Christ as a "divine deception" meant to trick the devil into releasing those held captive by death and Hades (a theme the liturgical hymns of Holy Week and Pascha later took up). In the final section, the Nyssen presents a description of the Sacraments of Baptism and the Eucharist, as St. Cyril does in his *Mystagogy*, but

---

30   Ibid., 101.
31   Ibid., 103.

again with an eye to apologetics. His primary concern is always for the proper formation of the catechumen, which entails correction of false conceptions of the Faith. For this reason, although the entire work is intended as a manual for catechists, it stands alone as both a catechism and a foundational theological treatise.

CHAPTER 9

Ascetical Works

THE VARIOUS WORKS ON ORTHODOX Christian spiritual life
comprise yet another large genre of patristic literature. Most of
these were written by and for monastic communities, although many
became standard reading for the laity as well. The authors are often
referred to collectively as the Neptic Fathers (from the Greek word
for "being watchful," *nēpsis*) called such because they are considered
to be the masters of keeping watch over their own souls. Later writers
describe these models of asceticism as "hesychasts"—those who seek
inner stillness (*hēsychia*), as well as "elders"—those more advanced
in spiritual practice. In the life of the Church, they even carry on the
vocation of prophecy through the acquisition of charismatic gifts
such as healing and clairvoyance.

There are multiple formats for ascetical literature. Some works
contain proverbs and stories connected to multiple monks or the
occasional fool for Christ. Others are collections of passages written by an individual saint, often arranged in centuries (groups of a
hundred). And others were originally written as manuals for fellow
monks. In later centuries we even find works written for seculars,
such as *The Unseen Warfare* by St. Theophan the Recluse. What all
these share in common is their intention of providing guidance to

the spiritual traveler. We will examine two such documents, both of which had a powerful and lasting impact upon the Orthodox Church.

The Sayings of the Desert Fathers

THE BIBLE CONTAINS SOME OF the most ancient collections of wisdom literature. The compilation of various aphorisms in Proverbs, Ecclesiastes, and other books set a pattern for the early Church, inspiring texts such as the "Alphabetical Collection" of *The Sayings of the Desert Fathers*. The history of the received text is complicated and uncertain. The monks whose sayings (apophthegmata) are contained therein began to flourish in the fourth century. The largest number of sayings originates from the areas of Scetis and Nitria, located south of Alexandria in Egypt, with some sayings coming from regions farther down the Nile. There, in the inhospitable conditions of the desert, men and women from diverse cultures and languages—Copts, Palestinians, Greeks, Romans and others—settled in caves or huts, cutting themselves off from the secular world to focus their attention on the attainment of salvation. Some chose to live as hermits, like St. Anthony the Great, while others settled around a wise elder—a spiritual father (*abba*) or mother (*amma*)—oftentimes working and praying together as a community (known as a skete). Monks who labored diligently in the spiritual life often became elders themselves, esteemed for their sagacity.

With the devastation of Scetis in about 407, the process of compiling the apophthegmata of the Desert Fathers likely began, as fear of losing the oral and written traditions became the catalyst for compiling the sayings. "Physical insecurity and a sense of moral decay gave impetus to the work, with the fear lest the great Old Men and their times be forgotten," writes Derwas Chitty.[1] Although many of

---

1   Derwas Chitty, *The Desert a City* (SVS Press, 1966), 67.

them may have first been heard in the Coptic tongue, the earliest edition of the "Alphabetical Collection" was written in Greek. Over a few centuries, translations appeared in Latin, Syriac, Armenian, Georgian, Arabic, and Ethiopian, which attests to their popularity. The most popular English translation of the "Alphabetical Collection" is that of Benedicta Ward, first published in 1975.[2] It is highly readable, even though it lacks a critical apparatus to accompany the text. A brief foreword gives some historical context, and a glossary of terms, chronological table, and two indices appear in the back. Following the original structure, the sayings are divided according to the first letter of the monastic figure's name (according to the Greek alphabet).

Although there is another collection of sayings from the Desert Fathers arranged according to various themes, we will use Ward's book and apply the same sort of schema to our examination, looking at three sayings each for the themes of repentance, humility, and remembrance of God. Our first theme is repentance. The Greek word *metanoia* implies that repentance involves a change of mind, a reorientation away from sin and back toward God. There are numerous sayings from the Desert Fathers that illustrate what repentance is, since it was understood not as a singular moment of conversion but as a continuous struggle with sin.

A saying from Abba Moses the Black, a former bandit who converted to Christianity and became a monk, reminds us that repentance is impossible unless we are brutally honest with ourselves: "'If the monk does not think in his heart that he is a sinner, God will not hear him.' The brother said, 'What does that mean, to think in his heart he is a sinner?' Then the old man said, 'When someone is occupied with his own faults, he does not see those of his neighbor.'"[3]

---

2   *The Sayings of the Desert Fathers: The Alphabetical Collection*, trans. Benedicta Ward (Cistercian Publications, 1975).

3   Ibid., 141.

His words remind us of Psalm 50/51:17, "A broken and contrite heart, these O God, you will not despise." The one who constantly acknowledges his own sins before the Lord will find favor, but the one who instead judges his brother's sins will be rejected, according to the evangelical commandment, "Judge not, that you be not judged" (Matt. 7:1).

Early collections of spiritual canons, such as those of St. Basil the Great or St. John the Faster, prescribed the length of penances (*epitimia*) for certain grave sins. Clergy would establish these periods of time, which entailed abstention from the Eucharist and additional prayers, in order for the sinner to reach the fullness of repentance and be healed of sin. A saying from Abba Poemen the Great confronts the concept of penances, revealing a more nuanced understanding of them:

> A brother questioned Abba Poemen, saying "I have committed a great sin and I want to do penance for three years." The old man said to him, "That is a lot." The brother said, "For one year?" The old man said again, "That is a lot." Those who were present said, "For forty days?" He said again, "That is a lot." He added, "I myself say that if a man repents with his whole heart and does not intend to commit the sin anymore, God will accept him after only three days."[4]

The goal of an epitimia, the saint reminds us, is to correct the sinner, not simply punish him. But he is not telling us something radically different from the other Fathers. For example, Canon 102 from the Council of Trullo (Quinisext) states:

> It behooves those who have received from God the power to loose and bind, to consider the quality of the sin and the readiness of the

---

4   Ibid., 169.

sinner for conversion, and to apply medicine suitable for the disease, lest if he is injudicious in each of these respects he should fail in regard to the healing of the sick man. For the disease of sin is not simple, but various and multiform, and it germinates many mischievous offshoots, from which much evil is diffused, and it proceeds further until it is checked by the power of the physician. Wherefore he who professes the science of spiritual medicine ought first of all to consider the disposition of him who has sinned, and to see whether he tends to health or (on the contrary) provokes to himself disease by his own behavior, and to look how he can care for his manner of life during the interval. And if he does not resist the physician, and if the ulcer of the soul is increased by the application of the imposed medicaments, then let him mete out mercy to him according as he is worthy of it. For the whole account is between God and him to whom the pastoral rule has been delivered, to lead back the wandering sheep and to cure that which is wounded by the serpent; and that he may neither cast them down into the precipices of despair, nor loosen the bridle towards dissolution or contempt of life; but in some way or other, either by means of sternness and astringency, or by greater softness and mild medicines, to resist this sickness and exert himself for the healing of the ulcer, now examining the fruits of his repentance and wisely managing the man who is called to higher illumination. For we ought to know two things, to wit, the things which belong to strictness and those which belong to custom, and to follow the traditional form in the case of those who are not fitted for the highest things, as St. Basil teaches us.[5]

The Fathers could approach these canons according to exactness (*akriveia*), which meant applying the canon exactly as worded, or according to pastoral application (*oikonomia*), which could refer to

---

5   *The Seven Ecumenical Councils of the Undivided Church*, NPNF/2 14:408.

shortening or dispensing with the penance if the clergyman felt it proper, or even lengthening it if a person refuses to repent.

Another question often asked about repentance concerns how often one should turn back to God. We find a suitable answer in the "Alphabetical Collection":

> A brother asked Abba Sisoes, "What shall I do, abba, for I have fallen?" The old man said to him, "Get up again." The brother said, "I have got up again, but I have fallen again." The old man said, "Get up again and again." So then the brother said, "How many times?" The old man said, "Until you are taken up either in virtue or in sin. For a man presents himself to judgment in the state in which he is found."[6]

Rather than fall into despair and assume eternal condemnation, a sinner should turn back as often as he or she falls, remaining confident that God is able and willing to forgive those who truly repent. This should stand out as a ray of hope for anyone struggling daily with temptation.

Another important theme in the Desert Fathers is that of humility. The word *humility* is derived from the Latin *humus*, referring to dirt. A humble person thus is one who descends down, like rain falling to the ground, thereby deflecting praise and emptying his or her soul of egotism and self-importance. The Desert Fathers exemplified this virtue, fleeing from pride as from the devil himself. Like Old Testament prophets such as Hosea, they would even demonstrate their lessons through unusual actions. Our first two sayings on the theme of humility illustrate this approach.

We begin with Abba John the Dwarf, who had withdrawn to Scetis to learn from a Theban elder:

---

6   *Sayings of the Desert Fathers*, 219–20.

His abba, taking a piece of dry wood, planted it and said to him, "Water it every day with a bottle of water, until it bears fruit." Now the water was so far away that he had to leave in the evening and return the following morning. At the end of three years the wood came to life and bore fruit. Then the old man took some of the fruit and carried it to the temple, saying to the brothers, "Take and eat the fruit of obedience."[7]

A common trope in ascetical literature is that humility can only be obtained through the practice of obedience, and we see this demonstrated here in the backstory of Abba John. He was renowned for his great humility and simplicity, which he gained through absolute obedience to his elder, even when the latter asked seemingly nonsensical things of him. That the dry branch eventually blossomed and bore fruit—an obvious miracle—becomes a testimony to Abba John's virtue, which he obtained after three long years of obedience.

Another beautiful illustration comes from Abba Moses the Black, known for his great humility:

A brother at Scetis committed a fault. A council was called to which Abba Moses was invited, but he refused to go to it. Then the priest sent someone to him saying, "Come, for everyone is waiting for you." So he got up and went. He took a leaking jug, filled it with water, and carried it with him. The others came out to meet him and said to him, "What is this, father?" The old man said to them, "My sins run out behind me, and I do not see them; and today I am coming to judge the errors of another." When they heard that, they said no more to the brother but forgave him.[8]

---

7   Ibid., 85–86.
8   Ibid., 138–39.

For St. Moses, a man cannot be humble if he is focused on the sins of his fellow man. We read in Scripture, "Pride goes before destruction, / And a haughty spirit before a fall" (Prov. 16:18). Pride is a satanic sin, an attitude that exalts oneself and condemns others. Forgiveness of others is the antidote this exemplar provides.

A next saying comes from one of the few women whose sayings are recorded in the "Alphabetical Collection":

> Amma Theodora said that neither asceticism, nor vigils, nor any kind of suffering are able to save, only true humility can do that. There was an anchorite who was able to banish the demons. He asked them, "What makes you go away? Is it fasting?" They replied, "We do not eat or drink." "Is it vigils?" They replied, "We do not sleep." "Is it separation from the world?" "We live in the deserts." "What power sends you away then?" They said, "Nothing can overcome us, but only humility." Do you see how humility is victorious over demons?[9]

The wise nun seems to attack the typical monastic practices, preferring humility to them all. But she is not saying they are useless: She understands that they are tools, a means to an end and not the goal themselves. The virtue of humility, on the other hand, conquers demons and invites God's grace. This is a lesson for all Orthodox Christians, a necessary corrective to a joyless asceticism that might result in vanity.

Our final theme is remembrance of God. This does not denote memories of God, either who He is or what He's done, but rather the constant awareness that we are standing in His presence. The famous model of monastic life, St. Anthony the Great, gives us a first glance at this practice:

---

9   Ibid., 84.

Someone asked Abba Anthony, "What must one do in order to please God?" The old man replied, "Pay attention to what I tell you: whoever you may be, always have God before your eyes; whatever you do, do it according to the testimony of the Holy Scriptures; in whatever place you live, do not easily leave it. Keep these three precepts and you will be saved.[10]

To find favor with God, the first step is to become acutely aware of Him. He is not elsewhere, cloistered off in His heavenly realm, but is everywhere present and filling all things. Once we become cognizant of this, we can put into practice the commandments of the Scriptures. The third recommendation—staying put—may seem uniquely applicable to monks (later codified with the monastic vow of stability); however, this is good advice for laypeople as well. We often have a tendency to flee stressful situations or to think the grass is greener on the other side. Making a commitment to remain and work through situations builds character and reinforces virtue, so long as we always remember God.

One of the sure ways to forget God is to shift our attention toward harmful practices, such as recollecting instances in which others have hurt us. "Abba Macarius [the Great] said, 'If we keep remembering the wrongs which men have done us, we destroy the power of the remembrance of God. But if we remind ourselves of the evil deeds of the demons, we shall be invulnerable.'"[11] Instead of reminding ourselves of past grievances, we should remember the ploys the demons use to destroy us. As St. Paul warns, "For we do not wrestle against flesh and blood, but against principalities, against powers, against the rulers of the darkness of this age, against spiritual *hosts* of wickedness in the heavenly *places*" (Eph. 6:12).

---

10   Ibid., 2.
11   Ibid., 136.

To complete our commentary on *The Sayings of the Desert Fathers*, we have an interaction with St. Joseph of Panephysis that indicates the heights to which remembrance of God can carry the monk:

> Abba Lot went to see Abba Joseph and said to him, "Abba, as far as I can I say my little [prayer] office, I fast a little, I pray and meditate, I live in peace, and as far as I can I purify my thoughts. What else can I do?" Then the old man stood up and stretched his hands toward heaven. His fingers became like ten lamps of fire and he said to him, "If you desire, you can become all flame."[12]

Abba Lot was the disciple of Abba Joseph and later became an elder in his own right. Yet here he seeks guidance, hoping to glean some bit of wisdom from his spiritual father so that he may advance. Abba Joseph's response is not to belittle him but to encourage him to journey further up and further in. The image of the saint's hand becoming beams of light is one we encounter elsewhere in Holy Tradition, such as with the famous conversation between Nicholas Motovilov and St. Seraphim of Sarov when the latter's face shone like the sun.[13] These and similar stories document real encounters with deification, evidenced by a revelation of the uncreated light of God—that very same light that emanated from Jesus Christ on Mount Thabor. In disclosing this truth to his disciple, Abba Joseph teaches us all to pursue holiness until the end.

The Ladder of Divine Ascent

THE BYZANTINE TRADITION PRESCRIBES ONLY a handful of nonliturgical texts to be read during divine services. These include

---

12   Ibid., 103.
13   *The Aim of Christian Life: The Conversation of St Seraphim of Sarov with N. A. Motovilov*, trans. John Philips (Saints Alive Press, 2010).

The Lausiac History by St. Palladius, various collections of homilies by the Fathers, and the synaxaria, which contains abbreviated lives of the saints or descriptions of important feast days. Another text that enjoys such recognition is *The Ladder of Divine Ascent* by St. John of Sinai, also dubbed "the Scholar" and "Climacus" (from *klimakos*, meaning "ladder"). This author flourished in the early seventh century, reposing in 649. He is commemorated by the Church twice annually, on March 30 and the fourth Sunday of Lent. After years of ascetical struggle at St. Catherine's Monastery on Mount Sinai, St. John eventually went into reclusion for a period of about twenty years. At the end of this time, his fellow monks convinced him to come out of seclusion and become their abbot, and he shared his spiritual wisdom with them. His book, which Orthodox monasteries today read during Lent each year, was considered a classic of spirituality even in its own time.

The text of *The Ladder* is divided into thirty chapters, a number St. John purposely chose to connote the age of Christ when he began His public ministry. Each chapter represents a step or rung on a ladder leading upward to perfection. (A famous twelfth century icon from St. Catherine's Monastery depicts this ladder, showing St. John leading his fellow monks up to Christ who awaits them at the top). In each chapter, St. John offers the reader practical advice and illustrative stories, peppered with biblical citations meant to both instruct and inspire. Various English translations have been published of the work, but we will cite the Holy Transfiguration Monastery edition, as it is the most commonly used in English-speaking monasteries. The editors also include an "Introduction," "A Sermon of Metropolitan Philaret on the Sunday of St. John of the Ladder," and a life of the saint written by Daniel, a monk of Raithu. Below we will examine only the first three steps, looking for application for non-monastics.

The first chapter is subtitled "On renunciation of the world." For the man or woman desiring to pursue a monastic vocation, this entails an actual departure from secular life. They leave the world and enter the monastery, rejecting the many concerns that characterize society at large. "Those who enter this contest," St. John writes, "must renounce all things, deride all things, and shake off all things, that they may lay a firm foundation."[14] Departure from the world must be absolute, or the monk will make no progress. But what of the married person who cannot leave behind the responsibilities of family life? Although such total renunciation is not possible for them, they too can make a good start, the saint tells us:

> Some people living carelessly in the world have asked me: "We have wives and are beset with social cares, and how can we lead the solitary life?" I replied to them: "Do all the good you can; do not speak evil of anyone; do not steal from anyone; do not lie to anyone; do not be arrogant towards anyone; do not hate anyone; do not be absent from the divine services; be compassionate to the needy; do not offend anyone; do not wreck another man's domestic happiness, and be content with what your own wives give you. If you behave in this way, you will not be far from the kingdom of heaven."[15]

These actions are a type of renunciation as well, but they are a fleeing from sin rather than from society.

The second step of *The Ladder* is closely connected to the first: "On detachment." Here St. John addresses a proper relationship with the material world, and with other people.

> The man who really loves the Lord, who has made a real effort to find the future kingdom, who is really pained by his sins, who is really mindful of eternal torment and judgment, who really lives in fear of

---

14   St. John Climacus, *The Ladder of Divine Ascent* (Holy Transfiguration Monastery, 2001), 6.
15   Ibid., 9.

his own departure, will not love, care, or worry about money, or possessions, or parents, or worldly glory, or friends, or brothers, or anything at all on earth. But having shaken himself of all his cares, and having come to hate even his own flesh, and having stripped himself of everything, he will follow Christ without anxiety or hesitation, always looking heavenward and expecting help from there.[16]

His instructions may seem either radical or hyperbolic, even for the monastic life. However, this is simply another way of restating what Christ says in the gospel: "If anyone comes to Me and does not hate his father and mother, wife and children, brothers and sisters, yes, and his own life also, he cannot be My disciple" (Luke 14:26); and "No servant can serve two masters. . . . You cannot serve God and mammon" (Luke 16:13). The monk cannot allow an earthly attachment to get in the way of following Christ. This is a valuable lesson for laypeople as well: As St. Peter remarked, "We ought to obey God rather than men" (Acts 5:29).

The third and last step we will consider is called "On exile." Although the term again may refer to retreat from society, St. John gives it a broader definition: "Exile means modest manners, wisdom which remains unknown, prudence not recognized as such by most, a hidden life, an invisible hardship, constant determination to love God, abundance of love, renunciation of vainglory, depth of silence."[17] Unlike Adam and Eve, who were involuntarily exiled because of sin, "the monk is a willing exile from his home"[18] He ventures out into the wilderness to flee from temptation and to struggle with himself. This is an experience that can and perhaps should be shared by every Orthodox Christian at some point in his or her life. It begins with a moment of clarity, an awakening to the call of God

---

16   Ibid., 11.
17   Ibid., 14.
18   Ibid., 15.

and repulsion of worldly vanity; and it finds fulfillment in letting go of those things that enslave us to sin—including relationships that become an obstacle to piety.

Before departing from step three, St. John adds a warning about dreams. Demons often transmit ideas and images into the mind during sleep to deceive the faithful. "He who believes in dreams is completely inexperienced," he concludes, "but he who distrusts all dreams is a wise man."[19] Having stated this caveat, the great ascetic continues his outline of spiritual life, gradually ascending from vice to virtue. The summit of the mount is the acquisition of the three supreme gifts of the Spirit: faith, hope, and love. These are a participation in God Himself, who enables sanctified humans to acquire true wisdom:

> He who has perfectly united his senses to God is mystically led by Him to an understanding of his words. But without this union it is difficult to speak of God. The indwelling Word perfects purity, and slays death by His presence; and after slaying death, the disciple of divine theology is illumined. The Word of the Lord himself, which is from God the Father, is pure and remains so eternally. But he who has not come to know God merely speculates. Purity makes its disciple a theologian, who of himself grasps the dogmas of the Trinity.[20]

As the fourth century monk Evagrius Ponticus famously wrote: "If you are a theologian, you will pray truly; and if you pray truly, you are a theologian."[21] With this we draw our inquiry on ascetical literature to a close, for nothing more can be said.

---

19   Ibid., 20.

20   Ibid., 227–28.

21   Evagrius the Solitary, "On Prayer: 153 Texts" in *The Philokalia: The Complete Text compiled by St. Nikodimos of the Holy Mountain and St. Makarios of Corinth,* vol. 1, trans. and eds. G. E. H. Palmer, Philip Sherard, and Kallistos Ware (Faber & Faber, 1979), 62.

CHAPTER 10

Liturgical Commentaries

T HE DIVINE LITURGY IS THE central act of worship in the Orthodox Church. It inducts the faithful into God's immediate presence, where He offers himself to His servants in the Eucharist. It is only natural that the Church Fathers would begin to contemplate the meaning of these services. As the structure of Christian worship emerged in the earliest period, certain elements became standard in all versions of the Divine Liturgy, such as litanies, consecration prayers, certain hymns (such as the Trisagion), and processions. Patristic commentators interpreted liturgical texts in the same way they did the Scriptures, finding literal and allegorical realities therein. These documents not only provide a snapshot of liturgical practice at a given point in history but also initiate the modern reader into the medieval mind of the Church.

St. Germanus of Constantinople

ONE OF THE EARLIEST AND most important Church Fathers to comment on the Divine Liturgy was St. Germanus, Patriarch of Constantinople from 715–730. During his reign he was known first as a defender of dyothelitism (the doctrine that Jesus Christ possesses both a divine and human will), which was under attack in the decades after the Sixth Ecumenical Council, and later as a staunch defender of veneration of sacred images when iconoclasm erupted in 726. For this, Emperor Leo III the Isaurian exiled him from his see, and he died several years later.

The *Historia Ecclesiastica* of St. Germanus presents a turning point in theological exposition on the Divine Liturgy. As Paul Meyendorff points outs, the earlier commentaries of St. Dionysius the Areopagite and St. Maximus the Confessor emphasized the eschatological horizons of the service, whereas St. Germanus represents the more innovative approach (for its time) of describing the service allegorically in terms of the life of Christ.[1] In the first portion of his commentary he symbolically defines the various architectural features of the temple and liturgical accoutrements. He then walks through the primary movements of the Divine Liturgy, explaining their meaning and interconnection. Following, we will examine passages from this work, using Meyendorff's translation in the SVS Press "Popular Patristics" series. The editor's introduction and commentary are quite helpful, making this an excellent resource for a study of the Church Fathers.

Saint Germanus uses the term for church (*ekklēsia*) to mean both the assembly of God's people and the temple they gather within. "The church is an earthly heaven in which the super-celestial God dwells and walks about."[2] It is greater than the tabernacle of Moses, having been foretold by the prophets and founded by the apostles. Within the church and temple there are various items that serve both a practical and spiritual purpose. The semantron (a long wood plank that is beaten with hammers to summon the faithful to worship) represents the trumpets of the angels; the apse in the eastern wall is both the

---

1   St. Germanus of Constantinople, *On the Divine Liturgy*, trans. Paul Meyendorff (SVS Press, 1985), 42.

2   Ibid., 57.

cave Christ was born in and the tomb He was buried in; and the holy table (altar) is the table of the mystical supper, the stone slab His body was lain on in the tomb, and the throne He sat upon in heaven.[3] Saint Germanus also describes features that no longer appear in most Orthodox temples, such as the ciborium (a canopy on pillars above the holy table) and the chancel barriers—low walls that were later replaced by the taller iconostasis.[4] He also explains the orientation of a Christian temple, which points toward the rising sun to signify Jesus, who is "the Sun of Righteousness" (Mal. 4:2).[5]

Next, St. Germanus describes the vestments and various liturgical items the clergy use. The poncho-like outer vestment called a *felōnion* is not cinched with a belt to denote "that even Christ thus went to the crucifixion carrying his cross."[6] The stole the priest wears (*epitra-chēlion*) is like a yoke around his neck, pointing to Jesus being "bound and dragged to his passion," while the wool stole worn over the shoulders of a bishop (*ōmoforion*) is the scarf Aaron wore. The saint then correlates the presbyters who serve the Liturgy to the twenty-four elders in Revelation 4:4–10 and the deacons to the angels who process around the heavenly altar.

The "bread of offering," today called *prosfora*, "signifies the superabundant riches of the goodness of our God, because the Son of God became man and gave himself as an offering and oblation in ransom and atonement for the life and salvation of the world."[7] The knife used to cut portions of this bread is called a lance—connecting it to the spear that pierced the side of Jesus—and the portions of bread removed show that Christ was led like a lamb to the slaughter (Is. 53:7). Wine and water are poured into the chalice as if from the

---

3   Ibid., 57–59.
4   Ibid., 59–63.
5   Ibid., 63.
6   Ibid., 67.
7   Ibid., 71.

side of the Lord, and now the "memorial of the mystical supper" is complete and ready for the Liturgy to follow.

Moving on, St. Germanus begins to unpack what occurs in the service itself. He begins with the antiphons, which at that time included Psalms 91/92, 92/93, and 94/95. These are "prophecies . . . foretelling the coming of the Son of God . . . [and] indicating his incarnation."[8] After these come the entrance of the Gospel book, signifying the entrance of Jesus into the world at his Nativity.[9] Then the singing of the Trisagion Hymn begins: "Holy God, Holy Mighty, Holy Immortal have mercy on us." This Trinitarian song, St. Germanus explains, also symbolizes the laity bringing gifts to the newborn Lord like the three magi, but instead of gold, frankincense, and myrrh they bring the virtues of faith, hope, and love. The bishop ascends his throne now, blesses the people with peace and is seated, signifying the completion of Christ's earthly ministry, His Ascension, and session at the right hand of the Father.[10]

Saint Germanus proceeds to explain the meaning of the *prokeimenon*, the Alleluia and censing, and the reading of the Gospel, breaking away for a moment from historical allegory. Mention of the Gospel prompts him to explain why there are four books bound as one, connecting each to the beasts in the vision of Ezekiel 1. This point in the service marks a transition from the Liturgy of the Word, focused on the biblical readings and culminating in the homily, to the Liturgy of the faithful, reaching its apex in the reception of the Eucharist. This second movement of worship begins with the majestic entry of the clergy into the temple with the offerings of bread and wine:

> By means of the procession of the deacons and representation of the
> fans, which are in the likeness of the seraphim, the Cherubic Hymn

---

8   Ibid., 73.
9   Ibid., 75.
10   Ibid., 77.

signifies the entrance of all the saints and righteous ahead of the cherubic powers and the angelic hosts, who run invisibly in advance of the great king, Christ, who is proceeding to the mystical sacrifice, borne aloft by material hands.[11]

This moment of pageantry simultaneously represents the burial of Jesus and His triumphal accession in Paradise. The sanctuary where the holy table stands now becomes "the heavenly altar," and the bishop takes his place before it to proclaim the prayers of consecration (the Anaphora). He "goes with confidence to the throne of the grace of God and, with a true heart and in certainty of faith, speaks to God."[12] Unlike Moses, he adds, the presiding clergyman speaks to God not through the cloud but with face uncovered. Within these prayers are recounted the whole economy of salvation leading up to the *epiklēsis*: a prayer to the Father to send down His Holy Spirit to change the bread and wine into the Body and Blood of Christ.[13] The Anaphora concludes with a commemoration of all the righteous departed.

The recitation of the Lord's Prayer follows at this point in the Divine Liturgy, and St. Germanus proffers an explanation of its contents.[14] He then abruptly ends his commentary with some final words about the Eucharist the people are about to receive:

> Then the priest exclaims, saying to all: I am a man of like passions with you, and I do not know the sins of each of you. "Look, see, behold God!" And "God is the Holy One who abides in the saints." The people respond saying, "One is holy, one is our Lord, Jesus Christ, with the God and Father and the Holy Spirit." For in the past,

---

11   Ibid., 87.
12   Ibid., 91.
13   Ibid., 97.
14   Ibid., 101–4.

Moses sprinkled the blood of the calves of goats, saying to the people, "This is the blood of the covenant of God" (Ex. 24:8). But now the Christ and God has given his own body and poured out and mixed his own blood, that of the New Covenant, saying, "This is my body and my blood, which is broken and poured out for the remission of sins." So henceforth with this understanding we eat the bread and drink the cup, as the Body and Blood of God, professing the death and resurrection of the Lord Jesus Christ, to whom be glory unto the ages. Amen.[15]

For the most part, the liturgical structure outlined in the *Historia Ecclesiasticus* is identical to the modern recension of the Divine Liturgy used in Byzantine practice. Scholars debate the origin of specific portions of these services as to whether they originated from vestiges of temple worship, from synagogue practice, from Jewish table prayers, or the imagination of early Christians. But from what we glean from St. Germanus, the meaning of liturgy is not derived from its constituent parts but from how they coalesce to become a participation in both the story of salvation below and the heavenly worship above.

St. Nicholas Cabasilas

A YOUNGER CONTEMPORARY OF ST. Gregory Palamas, St. Nicholas Cabasilas was an ardent supporter of the hesychastic movement. Scholars debate what his actual role was within the Church—whether as clergyman or lay theologian—but his writings remain an exquisite exposition of the Orthodox Faith. In *A Commentary on the Divine Liturgy*, his theological prowess and profound analysis are brought to bear, capturing the beauty and import of Byzantine worship in the

---

15   Ibid., 105.

days before the fall of Constantinople. An English translation by J. M. Hussey and P. A. McNulty, originally published by the Society for Promoting Christian Knowledge in 1960, has since been published by St. Vladimir's Seminary Press. The introduction by R. M. French outlines the Divine Liturgy as it looked in the fourteenth century and offers some additional information about how St. Nicholas understood the service.

With his introductory remarks, St. Nicholas states that the primary goal of the Divine Liturgy is the transformation of bread and wine into the Body and Blood of Jesus Christ: "Its aim is the sanctification of the faithful, who through these mysteries receive the remission of their sins and the inheritance of the kingdom of heaven."[16] All the various components of the service are directed toward this end, including "the prayers and psalms, as well as sacred actions and forms."[17] Expanding on this, he synthesizes the (by this time) traditional allegorical approach with a more pragmatic theological assessment. The service traces the deeds and sufferings of the Lord, inviting the worshipper to embark on a historical journey; but the hymns, prayers, and scriptural readings also "turn us towards God and obtain for us pardon for our sins . . . [and] make God look favorably upon us, and draw to us that outflowing of mercy which is the result of expiation."[18] The faithful are not aloof from the service, mere passive observers, nor are they simply reenacting past events; they are being sanctified through direct participation in God's goodness. The remainder of the introduction explains the meaning of the preparation of the bread prior to the Divine Liturgy.

In the second part of his commentary, St. Nicholas investigates the meaning of the Liturgy of the faithful. The high point of this half of

---

16   St. Nicholas Cabasilas, *A Commentary on the Divine Liturgy*, trans. J. M. Hussey and P. A. McNulty (SVS Press, 1997), 25.

17   Ibid., 25–26.

18   Ibid., 26.

the service is the appearance of the Gospel book in time for the readings. First the priest holds it aloft, "symbolizing the manifestation of the Lord, when he began to appear to the multitudes."[19] Now "the prophetic texts cease" and the Trisagion Hymn is sung to praise the Trinity, made possible because "the Savior revealed himself to us." This demonstrates "the harmony of the Old and New Testaments" and "that angels and men form one Church, a single choir, because of the coming of Christ who was of both heaven and earth."

The third and fourth sections of the commentary describe the Liturgy of the faithful, moving from the Great Entrance with the gifts of bread and wine through the recitation of the Nicene Creed and to the Anaphora. In pondering the miracle of the Eucharist, St. Nicholas explains the meaning of the offering:

> The Lord was not satisfied with sending the Holy Spirit to abide with us; he has himself promised to be with us, even unto the end of the age. The Paraclete is present unseen because he has not taken human form, but by means of the great and holy mysteries the Lord submits himself to our sight and touch through the dread and holy mysteries, because he has taken our nature upon him and bears it eternally. Such is the power of the priesthood. Such is the Priest—for after once offering himself, and being made a sacrifice, he did not end his priesthood, but is continually offering the sacrifice for us, by virtue of which he is our advocate before God forever. And therefore it was said of him: "You are a priest forever" (Ps. 110:4). This is why it is impossible for the faithful to be in any doubt about the consecration of the offerings, or of the other mysteries, if they are carried out rightly and with the prayers of the priests.[20]

---

19   Ibid., 59.
20   Ibid., 71.

After this wonderful assessment, he feels it necessary to answer certain polemics coming from the Latins who claim that the invocation of the Holy Spirit (*epiklēsis*) is unnecessary for the consecration of the Eucharist, or even blasphemous. After offering a protracted rebuttal to this accusation, he finally points out that one of the liturgical prayers of the Latin Mass, read after the consecration, asks God to allow His angels to carry up the Gifts to the heavenly altar, implying that the "words of institution" (i.e., when the priest says "this is the body . . . etc.") must not be sufficient to effect the change, hence requiring an additional prayer. Of course, modern liturgical scholarship has shown that most early versions of the Anaphora contained an *epiklēsis*, including the earliest Roman texts—information St. Nicholas did not have ready at hand. But his apologetic for Holy Tradition gives us a glimpse at how Byzantine theologians viewed the Roman Catholic Church of their time and responded to polemics.

Before describing the final prayers of thanksgiving, St. Nicholas inserts a theological parenthesis which describes the efficacy of the eucharistic service upon the faithful, both living and departed. On the one hand, those who have reposed with "purity of heart, love of God, desire for the sacrament, zeal for communion, a glowing ardor, a burning thirst" receive benefit in their souls, for all these characteristics are spiritual and not merely bodily.[21] Whereas, on the other hand, the living sometimes gain nothing from receiving the Eucharist due to their sinfulness. The dead are beyond sin, and if their inclination in life was toward virtue, "they are better disposed for communion with the Savior, not only than the majority of the living, but also than they would themselves have been if they were still in the flesh."[22] Offerings for the departed, a Jewish custom attested to at least as early as 2 Maccabees 12, find their justification in the defense

---

21   Ibid., 96–97.
22   Ibid., 101.

St. Nicholas Cabasilas gives. This is just one example of how *A Commentary on the Divine Liturgy*, although written in the Late Byzantine era, is both ancient and wonderfully contemporary in its themes, presentation, and writing style. A perfect companion to it is his second major work, *The Life in Christ*, which gives a detailed explication of the Sacraments in relationship to the overall Christian life.

CHAPTER 11

Hagiography

THE BIBLE CONTAINS NUMEROUS STORIES about righteous men and women. Their heroism was not wrought in struggle for perishable glory but for the truly imperishable glory that comes from fidelity to God. A large portion of Genesis tells the story of Joseph, an example of chastity. We read of Job, whose patience and longsuffering brought him face-to-face with God in the whirlwind. There are the accounts of prophets such as Samuel, Nathan, Elijah, and Elisha who spoke for God and performed miracles in His name. And in the New Testament, the Book of Acts chronicles the earliest missionary endeavors of the apostles and the many signs associated with their ministry. These biblical accounts of holy ones—*agioi* in Greek, *sancti* in Latin, or "saints" in English—were the model for the earliest Christian stories about the Church's heroes. This genre later became known as hagiography, or lives of the saints.

In the Greco-Roman world, historians proposed methods for researching and writing vitae of famous people. Collections such as Plutarch's *Lives of the Noble Greeks and Romans* are considered classics of the genre. These biographies trace the rise and fall of important figures, recording their virtuous deeds as well as their sinister ones. As the discipline of historiography continued to evolve, it was classified as a proper science. Scholars from the Enlightenment until now have envisaged their craft as an objective quest for data and a scientific reconstruction of the past. When they examine the life of an early Christian saint, they compile information from as many sources as possible, from contemporaries or near contemporaries, and then try to paint a picture based on this evidence. They further elaborate this image by using other evidence, such as archaeological finds. The project sometimes yields interesting results, but just as often, modern agendas influence the outcome of such projects, and saints revered by the Church may be recast as villains in these new narratives. Still, the myth of objectivity persists, and the historian's awareness of his or her own biases may be clouded by the gravity they ascribe to the quest.

In comparison, hagiography is a very different sort of literature with different intentions. In a sense, it is entirely eschatological: The life of a Christian is refracted through the lens of eternity. Like Orthodox iconography, which depicts the saint not in a naturalistic sense but as they exist in the ever-dawning age to come, so hagiography reveals the saint at the zenith of his or her spiritual journey. Past mistakes are not necessarily glossed over or ignored but are understood in light of that gradual movement toward theosis, which is only fully realized at one's denouement. This is because hagiography is meant to inspire the reader and to spur him on to greater heights. A sinner who sees himself as the prodigal son also imagines himself capable of returning home to the Father, and the downtrodden pilgrim who recognizes something of her own struggle in poor Lazarus is given hope for eternal respite. The lives of the saints introduce us to recurring patterns in the spiritual life. In a sense, all hagiography is a benchmark, a standard by which Christians measure their progress and set their sights on attaining Paradise.

The genre of hagiography may be divided into two categories. The first is represented by the various synaxaria. These are abbreviated compilations of saints' lives corresponding to the Menologion (annual cycle of festal and fasting days), intended to be read liturgically or devotionally. These exist in a state of flux, so to speak, as they are constantly being edited. For example, several collections exist from the Byzantine era. In Russia, St. Dimitri Rostov edited and published his own edition. And in the late twentieth century, Simonopetra Monastery on Mount Athos released their own version, which has since been translated into English. More abbreviated editions also exist, such as the *Prologue of Ohrid* by St. Nikolai of Žiča. The fluidity of these collections points to their utility: They are meant to inspire the faithful, not necessarily represent exhaustive historical narratives (particularly according to an empiricist interpretation of such). The integration of legendary accounts or repetition of tropes from other lives is not a bug but a feature, meant to challenge our modern chauvinism and bolster our trust in "things not seen" (Heb. 11:1).

The second category of hagiography is more complex, consisting of longer biographies about specific individuals, often written by those who knew the saint personally or who received a thorough synopsis from someone who did. The most noteworthy versions of such accounts are written by other saints and therefore are truly patristic texts. We will examine two biographies from this category: *The Life of St. Mary of Egypt* by St. Sophronius of Jerusalem and *The Life of St. Symeon the New Theologian* by St. Niketas Stethatos.

Life of St. Mary of Egypt

THE BIOGRAPHY OF ST. MARY (†522) is unique in that it is situated within a firsthand account from a hieromonk called St. Zosimas. In the initial part of his account, he describes his own monastic struggles and what eventually led to his first encounter with St. Mary. Then, through their conversation, she outlines her life story. However, this entire narrative is embedded in a larger one that St. Sophronius of Jerusalem (†638) told a century later, having received it from the monks at a monastery near the River Jordan where St. Zosimas had labored. This custody of transmission would not meet the litmus test of many secular historians, yet it certainly reflects the manner in which the Scriptures were passed down—a process the work of the Holy Spirit ensures. The popularity of *The Life of St. Mary of Egypt* in the Church bears witness to its inspirational character. In the Byzantine monastic liturgical cycle, the entire work is prescribed to be read aloud in the temple during the Matins (Orthros) and "Great Canon of St. Andrew of Crete" in the fifth week of Lent. Many parishes also follow this rubric.

Multiple contemporary English translations of the text have been published, all translated from languages other than the original Greek, including Slavonic, Latin, and Old English. One of the more popular versions English-speaking Orthodox parishes use devotionally, which we will cite below, is printed by Holy Trinity Monastery in Jordanville, New York.[1] Like some other editions, this volume also contains the complete "Great Canon." Although it does not contain an introduction or any critical apparatus, it serves the purpose of introducing the reader to the life of this great saint.

Saint Sophronius begins his tale by introducing us to St. Zosimas, whom he calls "a priest of holy life and speech, who from childhood had been brought up in monastic ways and customs."[2] Whether he literally was "taken from his mother's breast" and then "handed over to the monastery," or whether this is hyperbolic or perhaps metaphorical (considering that many monastic sayings and canons reveal a strong aversion to receiving beardless youth into the monasteries), is hard to say. Regardless, we are to understand that by age fifty-three

---

1   "The Life of our Holy Mother Mary of Egypt" in *The Great Canon: The Work of Saint Andrew of Crete* (Printshop of St. Job of Pochaev / Holy Trinity Monastery, 2005).

2   Ibid., 81.

St. Zosimas had become an experienced ascetic, such that he desired a more rigorous *podvig* (spiritual labor) to further test and purify him. Implied in the text is perhaps a nascent battle with pride, to which his encounter with St. Mary will provide the antidote.

After relocating to the monastery at the edge of the Jordanian wilderness, St. Zosimas began to follow the rule established there, which included a unique Lenten practice. All but a few monks would depart into the desert at the beginning of the Great Fast, taking some small amount of food with them. Praying and sleeping in the open, they would often survive off the plants growing there. And if any monk encountered another he would flee, hoping not to disturb his solitude. On Palm Sunday they would return to the monastery in time for Holy Week and the celebration of Pascha. On his first such adventure, St. Zosimas walked for twenty days before settling. While chanting the service of the Sixth Hour, he suddenly spied a person standing on a nearby hill. Even from that distance he could make out that the person was naked, with dark skin and shoulder-length white hair. The creature fled from him, and he pursued. Then he cried out, "Why do you run away from an old man and a sinner?"[3] Standing with her back toward the monk, she replied:

> Forgive me, for God's sake, but I cannot turn towards you and show you my face, Abba Zosimas. For I am a woman and naked as you see, with the uncovered shame of my body. But if you would like to fulfill one wish of a sinful woman, throw me your cloak so that I can cover my body and can turn to you and ask for your blessing.[4]

Saint Zosimas was terrified—not because she was a woman but because she called him by name. After throwing his cloak to her, he

---

3   Ibid., 84.
4   Ibid.

approached and asked her blessing. Quickly she proved herself capable of impossible feats, accurately describing his life and even reading his thoughts. Convinced of her sanctity, St. Zosimas convinced her to convey her story to him.

From this point until almost the end of the book, St. Mary describes the events that led to her retreat into the desert, beginning at age twelve when she left her home in rural Egypt for the allure of big-city life in Alexandria. She made a living by begging and spinning flax but spent her nights immersed in sexual debauchery. She lived like this for seventeen years (almost to age thirty), becoming addicted to perversity. "Then one summer," she explains, "I saw a large crowd of Lybians and Egyptians running toward the sea."[5] They were boarding a boat set for Jerusalem to celebrate the Feast of the Exaltation of the Cross and to venerate this miraculous wooden relic. Her curiosity piqued, she offered the sailors the payment of her body if they would let her accompany them on the voyage. But her fornication did not cease when they dropped anchor: She spent the days prior to the feast day seducing lads in Jerusalem.

When the holiday came, St. Mary tried to enter the temple with the other pilgrims to see the relic, but an invisible force prevented her. After several failed attempts, she realized that God had barred her entry because of her impurity. This was the crucial moment of self-realization that led to her repentance. Weeping, she looked up at an icon of the Theotokos on the porch and prayed to her, "Rightly do I inspire hatred and disgust before your virginal purity; but I have heard that God who was born of you became man on purpose to call sinners to repentance."[6] Asking for the Holy Virgin's assistance, she vowed to abandon her sinful life and go wherever she would be led. Feeling assurance of God's forgiveness, she entered the temple

---

5   Ibid., 87.
6   Ibid., 89–90.

without being hindered, received the Eucharist, and exited. Then, as she looked up again at the icon, she heard the words, "If you cross the Jordan you will find glorious rest."[7]

The holy woman tells St. Zosimas that she spent the next seventeen years fighting both her passions and the austere environment of the desert before beginning to experience some measure of peace. At the time of their meeting, she calculates it has been forty-seven years since she left the world. As their conversation continues, St. Zosimas notices that she quotes Holy Scripture, which prompts him to ask if she has copies of the texts at hand. She responds, "Believe me, I have not seen a human face ever since I crossed the Jordan, except yours today."[8] Her knowledge of the Bible, she adds, is taught by God.

Before she departs, St. Mary gives the monk some instructions. He is not to tell anyone of this encounter yet. After one year, when the Great Fast comes again, he should not leave the monastery with the others but remain until Thursday of Holy Week (when the Mystical Supper is commemorated liturgically). Then he should bring some of the Eucharist from the Divine Liturgy with him and cross the Jordan once more in order to commune the old woman. When, after a year, Lent begins, a sudden sickness prevents St. Zosimas from departing with the others; but he recovers by Holy Week. After the service, he walks down to the river with the Sacrament and some food. Saint Mary eventually appears on the opposite shore and walks across the water to meet him on the other side. She receives the Eucharist with joy and eats a few pieces of the food (accepting his hospitality). Before she traverses the river, she again instructs him to return to where they first met in one year when the next Lenten period begins. There he will see her one last time.

---

7   Ibid., 90.
8   Ibid., 93.

Another year passes and St. Zosimas heads into the desert to see St. Mary. However, he finds only her dead body. Next to her is written in the sand, "Abba Zosimas, bury on this spot the body of humble Mary," along with the date she died (the same day she had received the Eucharist, which was a twenty-day walk in distance).[9] Fulfilling her dying wish, he finds an old piece of wood and attempts to dig a grave, but the ground is too hard. Fear grips him when a lion suddenly appears by the body, but the beast begins to lick her feet as if greeting an old friend. Saint Zosimas asks the lion to dig the grave, and the creature obliges, using his paws to break up the soil. Afterward, the lion departs into the wilderness, and the monk returns to his monastery. Concluding this amazing account, the narrator St. Sophronius adds:

> May God who works amazing miracles and generously bestows gifts on those who turn to Him with faith reward those who seek light for themselves in this story; who hear, read, and are zealous to write it; and may He grant them the lot of blessed Mary together with all who at different times have pleased God by their pious thoughts and labors.[10]

The Life of St. Mary of Egypt is remarkable for a few reasons. First, it provides spiritual edification for Christians, especially those who have fallen into grave sins and despaired of salvation. The saint shows a way back to God through repentance and ascetical mastery of the passions. Second, it gives the modern reader a glimpse of life in the early Church, connecting it with practices still prevalent today. And third, it is beautiful from a literary standpoint and quite enjoyable to read. There are many sharp contrasts throughout. Saint Zosimas is an ascetic from youth and St. Mary a sinner, yet she reaches greater

---

9   Ibid., 96.
10   Ibid., 98.

heights of sanctity than he. He is fully clothed in a tunic and outer cloak, and she is naked yet adorned with the grace of the Spirit. He is a priest who offers blessings on behalf of Jesus Christ, yet he insists that St. Mary offer him the blessing instead. The entire tale is intended to instill both humility and hope in its readers. A classic of Orthodox Christianity, it holds a special place within Holy Tradition.

Life of St. Symeon the New Theologian

SAINT SYMEON THE NEW THEOLOGIAN was a pivotal figure in the latter half of the Byzantine period. He lived from 949–1022, a time when the imperial city of Constantinople was engorged by riches and tainted by the laxity of the average Christian. Born into a noble family, he decided to abandon life at court after meeting St. Symeon the Studite, an elder at the famous Stoudios Monastery. The ascetic asked his young new disciple to wait until he was older before entering the urban monastery. At age twenty-seven, St. Symeon finally left the world to embark on his new vocation. After a short time, his elder advised him to depart for the nearby St. Mamas Monastery where he would eventually be tonsured a monk, ordained a priest, and elected abbot. But the strict mode of life he imposed on the monks led many to rebel against him, and some even appealed to Stephen, the Metropolitan of Nicomedia. The hierarch instigated an investigation into the hieromonk, eventually bringing accusations to the synod of bishops against him. They maligned him for speaking of his own mystical and charismatic experiences, and they felt challenged by his attack on laxity within the Church. Finally, in 1009 he was exiled, taking residence in a small coastal village. A supporter there offered him a defunct chapel dedicated to St. Macrina, which he repaired and converted into a monastic skete. He remained there until his death.

Saint Niketas Stethatos was a young monk at the Stoudios Monastery who met St. Symeon close to the end of his life. Saint Symeon would send him his various writings for editing, which were later collected into eight large volumes. About thirty years after St. Symeon's death, St. Niketas undertook to publish a biography of his life, augmenting his own memories with biographical information from the great man's works and documented eyewitness accounts. This data was then interwoven with standard hagiographical tropes and numerous biblical citations to create a detailed work intended for spiritual elucidation. A recent critical edition of this biography has been published as part of the Dumbarton Oaks Medieval Library.[11] Editor Richard Greenfield provides the original Greek text parallel to his English translation, which is supplemented by a thorough introduction and substantial endnotes. As the work is very long, we will examine only chapters 68–71, which recount his mystical encounter with the Lord.

The event takes place just after St. Symeon's resignation as abbot of St. Mamas Monastery and prior to his exile. Having handed over the administration of the community to Fr. Arsenius, he concentrated his attention on hesychasm. "On one occasion, while he was standing in prayer and conversing with God," St. Niketas writes, "he saw with his intellect [*nous*] the air start to shimmer, and although he was inside his cell, he seemed to be outside in the open air."[12] A light began to shine from above, and the building around him seemed to disappear. The light he first perceived from afar became increasingly brighter, filling his mind and body with "joy and tears from the sweetness that emanated from it."[13] His whole being seemed to become as "fire and light," and then he heard a voice proclaim, "This is how it has been determined that the holy ones who are alive and who remain are to

---

11   Niketas Stethatos, *The Life of Saint Symeon the New Theologian*, ed. and trans. Richard P. H. Greenfield (Harvard University Press, 2013).

12   Ibid., 155.

13   Ibid., 157.

be transformed at the last trumpet, and this state caught up, as Paul says" (referencing 1 Thess. 4:17).

Saint Symeon's body began to seem like "a shadow or some immaterial substance," still tangible but no longer weighed down by the physical forces of this world. The voice again spoke, saying, "After the resurrection in the age to come, this is how all the saints will be incorporeally clothed with spiritual bodies."[14] Each person will be either lighter, ascending close to God, or heavier, sinking down: "And by this means each will have their station, rank, and intimacy with God established at that time." This eschatological vision continued for hours. Then, just as suddenly as it had begun, he "found himself back inside his cell in the same manner and form as before, entirely human."[15]

As is often the case in the lives of the saints, the incredible theophany St. Symeon experienced would be preparation for an ensuing hardship. It was not long after that the ecclesiastical authorities would persecute him and force him out of St. Mamas Monastery. But from his exile at St. Macrina's chapel, he would continue to plunge deeper into the hesychastic life and guide his disciples from afar. Thirty years after his death, the Church would exonerate him and bring his body back to Constantinople with great fanfare. His direct experiences of God would inspire beautiful poetry and profound ascetical texts: writings that would also become crucial in the hesychasm debate sparked by Barlaam in the fourteenth century. The visions documented in his biography by St. Niketas continue to be a source of inspiration for Orthodox Christians striving to understand theosis and the encounter with God's uncreated light.

---

14   Ibid., 159.
15   Ibid., 161.

CHAPTER 12

Hymnography

THE LITURGICAL CYCLE OF THE Orthodox Church is replete
with hymns, some (such as "O Gladsome Light") even dating back to the ante-Nicene era. But the bulk of hymnography was
composed during the Byzantine period. Some of our hymns are the
work of known saints, such as St. John Damascene, St. Theodore the
Studite, St. Joseph the Hymnographer, St. Theophanes the Confessor, and St. John Koukouzelis. Yet the vast majority remain anonymous, the work of brilliant artisans, most of whom were monastics.
For a majority of laypeople, these poetic writings remain their only
foray into the patristic mind—albeit, one of the most sublime and
theologically sound means to digesting Holy Tradition. The words
that comprise the current redaction of Byzantine hymnography have
undergone a gradual and stringent filtering process. Time, practice,
and prayer act as a sieve, allowing only the best to remain. Throughout this corpus are hidden quotes from the Church Fathers, summaries of conciliar decrees, explanations of theological concepts, and
allusions to important historical events. It has been said that someone
who chants every service at a monastery for an entire year, remaining
attentive at all times, receives the equivalent of a doctoral degree in
Orthodox theology.

Two of the most famous hymnographers are St. Romanus the Melodist and St. Kassiani the Nun. Between them they wrote hundreds of hymns. It is a testament to the filtering process of the Church that, despite the great reverence held for these two saints, only a handful of their works were eventually included in the final crystallization of Byzantine worship contained in books like the *Octoechos, Triodion, Pentecostarion,* and twelve volumes of the *Menaia*. We will briefly examine their lives and then examine a well-known hymn by each.

St. Romanus the Melodist

ONE OF THE EARLIEST BIOGRAPHIES of St. Romanus is found in the *Menologion of Basil II*. It reads, in its entirety:

> The venerable Romanus was from Syria and became a deacon of the holy church of Berytos. Arriving in Constantinople in the reign of the emperor Anastasios, he went and settled in the church of the most holy Theotokos in the *ta Kyrou* district, where he received the gift of the *kontakia*. In piety he would celebrate and pass the night, praying during the vigil at Blachernae, before returning to *ta Kyrou*. On one of these nights, the most holy Theotokos appeared to him while he was asleep, and gave him a paper scroll and said, "Take this paper and eat it." It seems the saint opened his mouth and swallowed the paper. Now it was the festival of Christ's Nativity. And, immediately, awakening from his sleep, he was astonished and glorified God. Thereupon he mounted the ambo and began to chant, "Today the Virgin gives birth to him who is above all being." He also composed nearly one thousand *kontakia* for other festivals before departing for the Lord.[1]

---

1   St. Romanos the Melodist, *Hymns of Repentance*, trans. Andrew Mellas (SVS Press, 2020), 9.

Other later accounts add that, prior to this miracle, the saint was unable to sing, or perhaps was even illiterate. As to additional information about his life, we know only that he flourished during the first half of the sixth century. But as can be seen in the above vita, what is best known about St. Romanus was his mastery of a new form of hymnody: the kontakion.

Derived from the Greek word for rod (*kontax*), a kontakion is structured around an opening prologue followed by many stanzas. They may have originally been written on long scrolls wrapped around a stick, hence their name. Some scholars posit that this format originated in Syria as a sort of "homily or sermon in verse that was chanted to music," which St. Romanus then perfected and introduced to Constantinople.[2] The only complete kontakion of the saint to remain in use today is the "Akathist to the Theotokos," which is chanted during the Great Fast. Within a few centuries, kontakia began to be replaced by the shorter canons, and what remained was the introductory prologue, which took on the name of the entire piece.

The hymn referenced above by Basil II comes from the kontakion St. Romanus wrote for the vigil on Christmas Eve. In the current Byzantine liturgical cycle, this opening hymn is chanted after the sixth ode of the canon; however, the remaining twenty-three stanzas of the original work, although extant, are no longer used. A complete translation can be found in the late Father Ephrem Lash's work, *Kontakia on the Life of Christ*. However, we will only examine the opening hymn familiar to all Orthodox Christians. As this is a short yet extremely profound text, it presents a perfect opportunity to drill down and examine the theology contained within, also looking to the original Greek for insights.

Immediately, the very first line of the hymn plunges us into the mystery of the Nativity: "The Virgin today gives birth to the

---

2   Ephrem Lash, *Kontakia on the Life of Christ* (HarperCollins, 1995), xxviii.

transcendent One." Saint Romanus, in his usual affection for the Theotokos, places her at the beginning of the song. Whereas many Byzantine works begin with "today" (*sēmeron*), he begins with *ē Parthenos*, "the Virgin." Yet he still includes the typical "today" afterward, a device meant to inform the hearer that he or she is not merely remembering a past event but participating in that exact moment through the Holy Spirit. It is a recapitulation of history— an anagogical view—moving us from a sensible *chronos* (linear time) and *choros* (physical location) toward a spiritual *kairos* (the precise moment) and *topos* (the precise place).[3] It is here that a worshipper meets "the transcendent One." The modifying adjective here, *hyperousion*, means something like "beyond being" or "above existence," employing apophatic language to describe the Son of God. If we say we ourselves exist, then He cannot exist; if we say He exists, we cannot. This is because His infinite, uncreated being is dissimilar to our finite, contingent being. We cannot fathom what it means to be God, or even God-made-man.

The second verse of the stanza presents us with personification, a common poetical mechanism: "and the earth offers a cave to the unapproachable One." The ground itself responds to its maker and makes a selfless sacrifice, giving the newborn Messiah a cave for His birthday. The tradition that the Theotokos gave birth in a cave rather than a stable is ancient, with references going back to at least the second century. In the hilly country near Bethlehem, keeping livestock in caves was a common practice. But the cave is not simply a historical datum; the image is redolent with symbolic meaning. The Lord has been born to die for the sake of His creatures. He comes forth from the womb into the tomb, prefiguring His death thirty-three years later. But again, He is not a mere man: His divine origin is

---

3   For a deeper discussion on this concept, see Archimandrite Vasileios, *Hymn of Entry* (SVS Press, 1997), *passim*. Also, my thanks to Richard Rohlin who suggested the addition of a "spatial" transition to that of a temporal one.

again referenced with the Greek word *aprositos,* meaning "unable to approach, reach, or come near," another apophatic term to emphasize the great mystery of the Incarnation. This is a paradox because many will approach Jesus of Nazareth during His earthly sojourn, yet none is able to come near His essence.

In the third verse of the hymn, St. Romanus succinctly compacts the entire Nativity account from the Gospel of Matthew into one sentence: "Angels with shepherds glorify Him; the wise men journey with a star." The celestial beings form a common chorus with earthly shepherds, singing a doxology (as the Greek states) to the Lord. The Fathers asserted that the holy angels are themselves members of the Church, and those who are redeemed by Christ become "equal to the angels" (Luke 20:36), thereby joining their ranks in the Kingdom of heaven. The scene is augmented by the arrival of wise men following a star. These are *magoi* ("magi"), a Persian word indicating their origin in the east. They studied the night skies seeking wisdom and portents of the future, but now a star has led them to the Creator of the whole cosmos. Also, as the phrase "journey with" implies, the star was not stationary but in motion, signifying the early Christian tradition that it was in fact another angel.

The final verse of this hymn wraps up our contemplation of this great mystery: "For our sake the eternal God is born as a little child." The contrast overwhelms us: The timeless God has entered into time, becoming man in order to save humankind. The adjective "eternal" (*aiōnōn*) means "of the ages" and refers to a deity greater than the many epochs He has created. It is the same word used in the Divine Liturgy, as in "unto the ages of ages." Interestingly, Origenists abused cognates of this term, contorting their meaning to insist that God's judgment will be limited only to the present age. This led them to believe that divine condemnation would eventually come to an end and that all would be saved. Yet the Nicene Creed refers only to a singular age to come (*tou mellontos aiōnos*)—a time inaugurated with the resurrection and dread judgment of all human beings. Of course, only God is eternal, beyond the ages; but He promises to establish an enduring epoch—a "kingdom without an end" (*basileias ouk estai telos*)—for those who love Him. For this reason He was born and died "for us men and for our salvation." Otherwise, our lives are a facade, freedom does not exist, and the last judgment is not a judgment at all. As St. Romanus understood, the Nativity of Christ marks the beginning of redemption for those who desire to be redeemed.

St. Kassiani the Nun

ALTHOUGH THE SECOND COUNCIL OF Nicaea (Seventh Ecumenical Council) in 787 denounced the heresy of iconoclasm, a second wave of persecution rocked the Church beginning in 815. A local synod issued a decree at the behest of Emperor Leo V the Armenian that ordered the removal of all religious imagery from churches (except for the cross). This action was challenged by many who were willing to suffer for the sake of right doctrine. Saint Kassiani came of age during this time and was shaped by these events. Born into an aristocratic family, she began to correspond as a teenager with St. Theodore the Studite (†826)—the great defender of icons—and received guidance from him on implementing a quasi-monastic lifestyle.[4] Once, she was even whipped as punishment for assisting iconodule monks in prison. After Emperor Theophilus began his reign in 829, he staged a "bride show," in which the most beautiful noblewomen were brought to court and paraded about. Saint Kassiani was selected for this show, which attests to her beauty. Perhaps to her great relief she was not chosen to be a bride and instead began to prepare herself to become a nun. The historical record then jumps

---

4   *Kassia: The Legend, the Woman, and Her Work*, ed. and trans. Antonia Tripolitis (Garland, 1992), xiv.

to 843, just after the end of iconoclasm, when we find her as abbess of a convent in Constantinople. Prior to her repose in 865, she composed nearly a hundred religious works as well as secular poems and collections of gnomic verses (maxims).[5] She spent her final days in quietude on the Greek isle of Kasos.

Saint Kassiani's most famous work is the hymn chanted as the doxastikon to the aposticha for Matins of Holy Wednesday (generally served on Tuesday evening). Special musical arrangements in both the Byzantine and Russian traditions accentuate the beauty of the text as well as its popularity. We will examine this succinct hymn in detail.

The first sentence reads: "Lord, the woman fallen into many sins, recognizing Your divinity, rises to the status of myrrhbearer, and mourning brings to You myrrh before Your burial." The hymn is directed to the Lord Jesus Christ rather than another divine Person or the Trinity. As the role of a doxastikon is to accompany the final doxology ("Glory . . . Now and ever . . .") at the end of a series of troparia, it is intended to praise God and glorify His mighty and saving acts. In this case, St. Kassiani does something unique: She invites us to praise Christ through the words and actions of the anonymous sinful woman mentioned in the Gospel narratives (see Luke 7:36–50; Matt. 26:6–13). Those gathered to worship in the temple are to identify themselves with this woman, admitting their own sins as they turn to the Lord. We also learn that through her repentance the woman is transformed, now becoming a prophetess who recognizes Jesus as divine and foresees His impending death. In advance, she mystically joins the ranks of the myrrhbearers who will later be the first witnesses to the empty tomb.

Saint Kassiani then shifts from the external circumstances to the inner monologue of the sinful woman: "Woe to me, she says, for night

---

5   Ibid., xviii.

holds for me the frenzy of intemperance, gloomy and moonless, a desire for sin." She laments her situation, realizing that her constant struggle with "intemperance" or "licentiousness" (*akolasias*) is not rational but "frenzy" or "madness" (*oistros*). It is an experience akin to a dark, moonless night, and her unquenchable desire is here described as *erōs*, a powerful attraction toward sin. The hearer is invited into the condition of the sinful woman's soul, thereby making connections with his or her own struggle with temptation.

The woman's repentance is represented by her tears of remorse: "Accept the springs of my tears, You who with the clouds gathered together the water of the sea; bend down to me, to the lamentations of my heart." Her weeping becomes a "fountain" (*pēgē*). The second clause employs the present participle *stemonizōn*, which some translations render as "gathering together." Its usage here seems to be a double entendre, as it comes from the noun *stemon*, which can refer to either the rudder of a ship or the warp in weaving with a loom. Hence its verbal cognate can refer either to "commanding / steering" (like the captain of a ship) or "weaving together," and it is possible St. Kassiani intends both meanings simultaneously: By His direct command, the Word of God made the cosmos and now continues to sustain the order of creation as he weaves together water from the sea to form the clouds above.

A paradox is at play here: The sinful woman asks the Creator of the clouds above to "bend down" to her, meet her in the midst of her struggle and hear the "lamentations" or "groanings" of her heart. She then adds a parallel verse with similar meaning, a device ubiquitous in Hebraic poetry such as the Psalms, adding, "You who made the heavens incline by Your ineffable humiliation." The word for "humility" here is *kenosis* or "self-emptying," which St. Paul uses in Philippians 2:7 to describe the Incarnation. These bold juxtapositions of Jesus as both divine King and humble slave became a frequent trope in Byzantine hymnography, finding expression as early as the second century with *On Pascha* by St. Melito of Sardis and theological warrant in the antinomies of St. Cyril of Alexandria. Paradoxical language is necessary if anything is to be said about "the mystery of Christ" (Eph. 3:4).

The sinful woman, in her spiritual dialogue with Christ, reveals what she will do next: "I will tenderly kiss Your sacred feet, I will wipe them again with the hair of my head: the feet whose sound Eve heard in Paradise in the evening and hid in fear." She recognizes the feet of Jesus as sacred (*achrantous*, meaning "undefiled" or "immaculate"). But these are not the feet of any mere man but of the Lord who walked in the "cool of the evening" in Eden, a direct reference to Genesis 3:8 (Septuagint translation). This revelation is often startling to modern hearers unfamiliar with the early patristic understanding about the "second Yahweh" or Angel of the Lord who appears in the Old Testament.[6] This figure has always been identified as Jesus Christ Himself, as no one can see the invisible Father and live (see Ex. 33:20; John 1:18). The woman anoints those same feet whose sound Eve heard; but whereas the "foretype" hid in shame, the antitype courageously approaches the Lord in repentance.

To conclude her hopeful lament, St. Kassiani has the sinful woman ask for forgiveness in her heart: "Who can measure the multitude of my sins and the depths of your judgment, my Savior of soul and body?" Her sins are beyond measurement, and the "judgments" or "verdicts" (*krimatōn*) are like a great abyss (*abyssous*), unfathomable. Even so, she cries out to her Lord as "my Savior," then refers to Him as *psychosōsta* or "soul-saver." In other words, Jesus Christ is, by nature, the one who can save souls; but in this instance the sinful woman asks that He become her personal Savior. He is not an impersonal god

---

6   For more information on this, see the following: Stephen De Young, *The Religion of the Apostles* (Ancient Faith Publishing, 2021); Andrei Orlov, *The Glory of the Invisible God: Two Powers in Heaven Traditions and Early Christology* (T&T Clark, 2021).

but the God who established a relationship with Adam and Eve, with the patriarchs and prophets, and is now seated in front of her in the home of the Pharisee.

With this, she finally makes her request: "Do not disregard me, Your servant: You whose mercy is without measure." She falls down before Him as a servant, or even a slave (*doulos*), ready to receive His command; but she also knows that His mercy is "without measure." This last statement is contrasted against her own sins which are "beyond measure." Christ is her only assurance of deliverance, the only one able to cure her "frenzy of intemperance" (as stated above). The woman does not merely seek a legal pronouncement—a pardoning of guilt—but healing of her sinful condition. Here the author, St. Kassiani, perfectly captures the Orthodox Christian understanding of human nature, distorted by corruption at the fall. Like a Second Eve, the woman with the alabaster flask reverses the condemnation through heartfelt contrition.

Conclusion

W E HAVE REACHED THE END of our exploration of the Holy
Fathers. This manual is not meant to be exhaustive in any
way, only to provide a useful methodology and a taste of the patristic library. My goal has been to encourage members of the Orthodox Church—nonspecialists—to read and learn from the Fathers
and to avoid misinterpreting them by imposing personal biases and
modernist presuppositions upon their works. As representatives of
Holy Tradition, their writings are an inheritance for every Orthodox
Christian endeavoring to "work out [their] own salvation with fear
and trembling" (Phil. 2:12). It is important to remember here that
the texts we have received should never be read in isolation from the
ascetical, liturgical, and sacramental life of the Church. When inte-
grated within a robust spiritual program, they can strengthen our
faith and inform our praxis. The journey toward theosis may seem
arduous, but we have the testimony of the Scriptures and the saints to
assure us that transformation in Christ Jesus is truly possible.

As mentioned in the introduction, my approach to reading the
Fathers is not based solely on academic analysis. As an Orthodox
Christian, I know the saints are my forebears and friends. They are
like a lamp and guide to the weary traveler. I have offered to you what
I have gleaned from my mentors and from my personal study of the
texts over many years. Whatever mistakes or omissions in the manual are my own; and wherever I have disagreed with other scholars

or interpreters is likely due to my confessional interpretation and attempt to adhere to the high standard of Orthodox Christian theology. I hope that the information you have learned will be helpful.

The next step in your exploration of the Church Fathers is to obtain a few works and begin reading. Appendix D offers a "Graduated Reading List," with suggested readings ranked by difficulty. The other appendices provide additional resources and information to assist you along the way. Older translations may be obtained online for free, but they usually lack any interpretive apparatus to provide further context. They may also reflect heterodox confessional or denominational biases, an issue less common in more recent translations. Newer translations are not necessarily pristine either, and they may sometimes reflect certain political or sociological biases. Without knowledge of the original languages, caution should be taken, especially if you are tempted to formulate some theological opinion from your reading. This is particularly true if your opinion seems to confirm your biases or if it challenges the general opinion of Orthodox clergy and scholars. We should always approach patristic texts with humility and an open mind.

As you begin your study of the Holy Fathers, remember to always begin with prayer: first to God, and then to the saint whose writings you are engaging that day. Take your time and read slowly, giving yourself ample time to decipher the text and tussle with its meaning. Most importantly, remember to put into practice the lessons you learn, lest the Fathers become an abstraction. May the Lord lead your exploration of the patristic treasury, that you may be enriched by the labors of His saints.

Glory to God for all things!

Footnote Abbreviations

ANF: Roberts, Alexander, and James Donaldson, eds. *The Ante-Nicene Fathers: Translations of the Writings of the Fathers Down to A.D. 325.* 10 vols. (1885–1887). Republished by Hendrickson Publishing in 1996. The text is public domain, and can be found at CCEL.org.

NPNF: Schaff, Philip, and Henry Wace, eds. *A Select Library of Nicene and Post-Nicene Fathers of the Christian Church.* 28 vols. in 2 series. (1886–1889). Republished by Hendrickson Publishing in 1979. The text is public domain, and can be found at CCEL.org.

SVS Press: St. Vladimir's Seminary Press

Timeline of the Church Fathers

Date (Anno Domini)	Event
30 / 33	Crucifixion and Resurrection of Jesus Christ
48–98	Composition of New Testament documents and *Didache*
107	Martyrdom of St. Ignatius of Antioch
108–124	Persecution by Emperors Trajan and Hadrian
144	Excommunication of Marcion
155	Martyrdom of St. Polycarp of Smyrna
166	Quartodeciman Controversy
177–180	Persecution by Emperor Marcus Aurelius
202–210	Persecution by Emperor Septimus Severus
202	Martyrdom of St. Irenaeus of Lyon
205	Origen appointed head of the Catechetical School
235–238	Persecution by Emperor Maximinus Thrax
250–251	Decian Persecution
257–260	Valerian Persecution
258	Martyrdom of St. Cyprian of Carthage
285	St. Anthony the Great flees to the desert

301	King Tiridates III of Armenia converts to Christianity
302–312	Diocletian Persecution
311	Donatist Schism begins
312	Conversion of St. Constantine the Great
313	Edict of Milan gives official status to Christianity
325	Council of Nicaea (First Ecumenical Council)
361–363	Persecution by Julian the Apostate
367	Encyclical of St. Athanasius listing canon of Scripture
379	Repose of St. Basil the Great
381	First Council of Constantinople (2nd Ecumenical Council)
398	St. John Chrysostom appointed Archbishop of Constantinople
410	Fall of Rome to the Visigoths
431	Council of Ephesus (3rd Ecumenical Council)
444	Repose of St. Cyril of Alexandria
449	Robber Synod of Ephesus
451	Council of Chalcedon (4th Ecumenical Council)
484	Founding of Mar Saba Monastery in Jerusalem
537	Consecration of Hagia Sophia in Constantinople
527	Founding of St. Catherine's Monastery on Mount Sinai
541–544	Jacob Baradaeus organizes Monophysite communities
553	Second Council of Constantinople (5th Ecumenical Council)
636–646	Muslim conquest of the Levant and Egypt
662	Repose of St. Maximus the Confessor
680–681	Third Council of Constantinople (6th Ecumenical Council)

692	Council at Trullo (Quinisext Council)
712	Repose of St. Andrew of Crete
726	Iconoclasm Controversy begins
749	Repose of St. John Damascene
787	Second Council of Nicaea (7th Ecumenical Council)
800	Charlemagne coronated in Rome
810	Pope Leo III bans addition of filioque to the Nicene Creed
843	Restoration of Icons
865	Conversion of Bulgaria to Orthodox Christianity
870	Conversion of Serbia to Orthodox Christianity
879–880	Fourth Council of Constantinople (Photian Council)
885	Mount Athos granted autonomous status
963	Founding of the Great Lavra on Mount Athos
988	Conversion of Kievan Rus
1014	Pope Benedict VIII inserts filioque into Roman creed
1022	Repose of St. Symeon the New Theologian
1054	Great Schism between Rome and Constantinople
1095	First Crusade begins
1204	Fourth Crusade sees sacking of Constantinople
1261	Latin occupation ends in Constantinople
1340	Founding of Holy Trinity Monastery near Moscow
1341–1351	Fifth Council of Constantinople (Palamite Council)
1439	Council of Florence
1453	Fall of Constantinople to the Ottoman Turks
1573–1581	Lutherans correspond with Patriarch Jeremias II
1596	Union of Brest-Litovsk and beginning of Uniatism
1672	Synod of Jerusalem

1724	Melkite Schism
1782	St. Nicodemus the Hagiorite publishes *Philokalia*
1794	St. Herman of Alaska arrives on Kodiak Island
1821–1832	Greek War of Independence
1848	*Encyclical of the Eastern Patriarchates*
1867	Repose of St. Philaret of Moscow
1872	Synod of Constantinople
1917	Fall of the Russian Empire to the Bolsheviks
1922	Dissolution of the Ottoman Empire
1938	Repose of St. Silouan the Athonite
1956	Repose (Martyrdom) of St. Nikolai of Žiča
1989–1991	Fall of Communism in Eastern Europe
1994	Repose of St. Paisios the Athonite

References and Resources

HISTORY

Kesich, Veselin. *Formation and Struggles: The Birth of the Church AD 33–200*. St. Vladimir's Seminary Press, 2007.

Louth, Andrew. *Greek East and Latin West: The Church AD 681–1071*. St. Vladimir's Seminary Press, 2007.

Meyendorff, John. *Imperial Unity and Christian Divisions: The Church AD 450–680*. St. Vladimir's Seminary Press, 2011.

Papadakis, Aristeides. *The Christian East and the Rise of the Papacy: The Church AD 1071–1453*. St. Vladimir's Seminary Press, 1994.

PATRISTICS

Blowers, Paul M., and Peter W. Martens, eds. *The Oxford Handbook of Early Christian Biblical Interpretation*. Oxford University Press, 2019.

McGuckin, John Anthony, ed. *The Westminster Handbook to Patristic Theology*. John Knox Westminster Press, 2004.

Veniamin, Christopher. *The Orthodox Understanding of Salvation*. Mount Thabor Publishing, 2013.

Zisis, Theodore. *Following the Holy Fathers: Timeless Guides of Authentic Christianity*. Translated by John Palmer. Newrome Press, 2017.

THEOLOGY

Cunningham, Mary B., and Elizabeth Theokritoff, eds. *Cambridge Companion to Orthodox Christian Theology*. Cambridge University Press, 2008.

Lossky, Vladimir. *Dogmatic Theology: Creation, God's Image in Man, & the Redeeming Work of the Trinity*. Translated by Anthony P. Gythiel. St. Vladimir's Seminary Press, 2017.

Romanides, John. *An Outline of Orthodox Patristic Dogmatics*. Translated by George Dion Dragas. Orthodox Research Institute, 2004.

Stăniloae, Dumitru. *The Experience of God: Orthodox Dogmatic Theology*. Translated and edited by Ioan Ionita and Robert Barringer. 6 vols. Holy Cross Orthodox Press, 1994–2016.

PHILOSOPHY

Blackson, Thomas A. *Ancient Greek Philosophy: From the Presocratics to the Hellenistic Philosophers*. Wiley-Blackwell, 2011.

Cavarnos, Constantine. *Orthodoxy and Philosophy*. Institute for Byzantine and Modern Greek Studies, 2003.

Graduated Reading List

LEVEL 1

1. St. Irenaeus of Lyon, *On the Apostolic Preaching*
2. St. Athanasius the Great, *On the Incarnation*
3. St. John Chrysostom, *Sermons on Marriage and Family Life*
4. St. Gregory the Theologian, *Festal Orations*

LEVEL 2

1. St. Ephrem the Syrian, *Hymns on Paradise*
2. St. Dorotheus of Gaza, *Discourses* or *"Various Soul-Profiting Instructions"*
3. St. John Damascene, *Three Treatises on the Divine Images*
4. St. Nicholas Cabasilas, *The Life in Christ*

LEVEL 3

1. St. Gregory of Nyssa, *The Life of Moses*
2. St. Isaac of Nineveh (the Syrian), *Headings on Spiritual Knowledge*

3. St. Cyril of Alexandria, *On the Unity of Christ*
4. St. Gregory Palamas, *The Triads*

LEVEL 4

1. St. Photius the Great, *On the Mystagogy of the Holy Spirit*
2. St. Symeon the New Theologian, *The Ethical Discourses*
3. St. Basil the Great, *Against Eunomius*
4. St. Maximus the Confessor, *On Difficulties in the Church Fathers* or *De Ambigua*

Patristic Series in English

ANTE-NICENE AND NICENE/
POST-NICENE FATHERS

This massive collection of translations was compiled, edited, and published by Protestant scholars Philip Schaff and Henry Wace from 1886 to 1900. The translations begin with the Apostolic Fathers and end with St. John Damascene in the East and St. Gregory the Great in the West. Numerous scholars contributed to the volumes, so the quality and utility of the introductions and footnotes vary greatly from section to section. The language is sometimes antiquated and may have strong Protestant colorings to it. However, the entire collection is now in the public domain and can be accessed for free online at the Christian Classics Ethereal Library (ccel.org).

POPULAR PATRISTICS SERIES

This series contains dozens of short texts intended for lay readers to gain an appreciation of the Fathers. SVS Press is the academic publishing house for St. Vladimir's Orthodox Seminary in Crestwood, New York. Although not every translator is Orthodox Christian, the editors (currently patristic scholar Fr. Bogdan Bucur, and previously Fr. John Behr) ensure that the editions are in line with Orthodoxy. Each publication in the series offers an introduction to the text and a critical apparatus to assist in reading. To date, volumes span from the second century to St. Symeon the New Theologian in the eleventh century.

FATHERS OF THE CHURCH: A NEW TRANSLATION

This ongoing series, first launched in 1947, is published by the Catholic University of America Press. There are many wonderful volumes of this series, with excellent introductions and footnotes, several of which are edited and translated by Orthodox Christians. However, the series also contains texts by authors not considered saints in the Orthodox Church, so caution is advised when selecting which to read.

ANCIENT CHRISTIAN WRITERS: THE WORKS OF THE FATHERS IN TRANSLATION

This ongoing series was first launched in 1946 by Roman Catholic patristics scholar Johannes Quasten. It began under Newman Press and was later continued by Paulist Press. The quality of the translations and introductions varies greatly from volume to volume, and caution is again advised regarding which texts come from Orthodox saints.

CLASSICS OF WESTERN CHRISTIAN SPIRITUALITY

Also published by Paulist Press, this series focuses on writings that reflect the spirituality of early Christianity. Again, the quality of the translations and introductions varies greatly from volume to volume, and caution is again advised regarding which texts come from Orthodox saints.

DUMBARTON OAKS MEDIEVAL LIBRARY

Dumbarton Oaks is a research institute affiliated with Harvard University. One of their concentrations is the Byzantine era; thus, they publish translations of select texts from this period through Harvard University Press. The "Medieval Library" series has several excellent volumes by the Fathers, with the Greek original text in parallel. However, this is a large collection with most volumes of interest only to scholars working in Byzantine or Medieval studies.

LOEB CLASSICAL LIBRARY

This massive collection of ancient and medieval texts was originally published by Heinemann (London) beginning in 1912 and was later taken over by Harvard University Press. Only a handful of volumes contain writings from the Greek and Latin Fathers, with parallel text in the original language. The introductions are not especially helpful, but the translations are sufficient. Perhaps the best use of these volumes is as a primer for those cutting their teeth on reading Greek and Latin along with the Fathers.

MONASTIC WISDOM SERIES

Cistercian Publications in Kalamazoo, Michigan (distributed by Liturgical Press) has been offering translations of texts by early Christian contemplatives since 1968. This series contains important texts from monastics such as St. Dorotheus of Gaza, St. Diadochos of Photiki, St. Isaac the Syrian, and others. They also publish works by modern scholars examining these ancient writers.

OTHER ORTHODOX PUBLISHERS

Occasionally, Orthodox presses publish patristic texts, such as St. Tikhon's Monastery Press (South Canaan, Pennsylvania), Holy Cross Orthodox Press (Brookline, Massachusetts), Holy Trinity Publications (Jordanville, New York), St. Herman Press (Platina, California), and others. Although they do not specialize in such content, or offer dedicated series of patristic texts, you can find some excellent translations from these sources.

Scripture Index

Subject Index

About the Author

ARCHPRIEST JOSEPH LUCAS IS THE rector of Christ the Saviour Orthodox Cathedral (Miami Lakes, FL), adjunct professor of theology at St. Thomas University (Miami Gardens, FL), and co-senior editor of *Rule of Faith Journal*. He received his PhD in theology at Radboud University (Netherlands) and his MDiv with Distinction in Patristics at St. Tikhon's Orthodox Theological Seminary (PA).

We hope you have enjoyed and benefited from this book. Your financial support makes it possible to continue our nonprofit ministry both in print and online. Because the proceeds from our book sales only partially cover the costs of operating **Ancient Faith Publishing** and **Ancient Faith Radio**, we greatly appreciate the generosity of our readers and listeners. Donations are tax deductible and can be made at **www.ancientfaith.com**.

To view our other publications,
please visit our website:
store.ancientfaith.com

Bringing you Orthodox Christian music, readings, prayers, teaching, and podcasts 24 hours a day since 2004 at
www.ancientfaith.com